ALL
MOMS
WORK

ALL MOMS WORK

*Short-Term
Career
Strategies for
Long-Range
Success*

Sharon Reed Abboud

Capital Ideas Series

CAPITAL
BOOKS, INC.
Sterling, Virginia

Capital Books, Inc.
P.O. Box 605
Herndon, Virginia 20172-0605

ISBN 13: 978-1-933102-68-9

Library of Congress Cataloging-in-Publication Data

Abboud, Sharon Reed.
All moms work : short-term career strategies for long-range success / Sharon Reed Abboud. — 1st ed.
p. cm. — (Capital ideas series)
ISBN 978-1-933102-68-9 (alk. paper)
1. Stay-at-home mothers—Vocational guidance. 2. Women—Employment re-entry. 3. Work and family. I. Title. II. Series.

HF5382.6.A23 2009
650.1085'2—dc22

2008049363

Printed in the United States of America on acid-free paper that meets the American National Standards Institute Z39-48 Standard.

First Edition

10 9 8 7 6 5 4 3 2 1

*I dedicate this book, with love,
to my four wonderful children:
Melissa, Jessica, Andrea, and Danny.*

CONTENTS

PREFACE

All moms work, whether as a stay-at-home mom, full-time working mom, volunteer, part-time employee, business owner, or consultant. I wrote this book to help readers discover new ideas for how, when, and if they want to work. It is meant to be an *actionable* resource—extensive website links are included to get you started on researching new career options. These website links are not all-inclusive—but merely a sampling of websites that you can use as a springboard for finding out other sources of information. As you read this book, you may want to keep a journal of your thoughts and notes about how to shape your own career and develop your own personal career plan.

My Story: Sharon Reed Abboud

I found out my husband and I were expecting our first child while I was working as a business journalist. Prior to that, I was an academic advisor at American University in Washington, DC. During my pregnancy I had a nine-month case of severe hyperemisis—which means nonstop nausea. My employer allowed me to telecommute from home, but after the baby was born, the company expected me to return there and work full time. While fully intending to go back to work while I was pregnant, after I had my baby, I just couldn't do it. After going back to work, the company wanted me to travel to conferences in Paris and Hawaii. My response was, "No way!" I even surprised myself with my reaction. Prior to having the baby, I could not imagine having such a response. Paris? Hawaii? These would have been dream trips. But my baby was very colicky, and I couldn't imagine how I could bring her along. Add to that, I didn't want to leave my baby at all to go to work every day. My life view had flip-flopped—my baby's smile was more important to me than any job or trip.

Fast forward . . . within the next six years I had three more babies. Like all of us, my babies, now children, are the joy of my life. And I don't regret any minute of being a stay-at-home mom.

I wrote freelance articles for magazines while my children were infants, and then after that revved up, I re-launched my career as a writer and career consultant. Along the way, I volunteered at my children's schools and in the community.

I live in a typical American suburb—probably half of my female friends and neighbors are stay-at-home moms. As everyone's children got older, I expected to see many of them go back to work full time. Rarely, however, did I see a mom have to return to the full-time workforce, unless that was her choice in terms of her professional goals. Instead, some moms were working part-time or telecommuting. Others started successful businesses. Some moms had become consultants or writers. All of these moms were finding creative and enterprising ways to continue their careers and make money.

The idea for this book began when I started researching this phenomenon and found it was happening throughout the country and in many other countries. Women today are taking hold of their own career planning, rather than being the hostage of former societal expectations of being either a full-time professional or a full-time stay-at-home mom.

All this said, however, I don't think it's better to be a stay-at-home mom or work full time—or own a business, work part-time, telecommute, or any other type of work setup. Ideally we all should be able to determine the work-life balance that is best for ourselves and our families. If you want to work and/ or need to work full time, however, you may want to find out about flexible work options in order to enable you to have more time for your family and a more ideal work-life balance.

If you do decide to stay home, this book will show you how to use short-term and long-range strategies for your career success. By following these strategies, you should be able to go back to work full time at a future date of your own choosing. You will have kept your network, taken steps to enhance your resume, and be up-to-date with your profession. Then you can sit back, relax, and enjoy your time at home with your children—knowing that you have taken the steps necessary for your future career success.

A Note to Dads

While there are a number of stay-at-home dads out there, this book is written primarily with the concerns of women in mind. That said, many of the career strategies in this book are applicable to both women and men. In 2006, there were an estimated 5.6 million stay-at-home mothers and 159,000 stay-at-home fathers, according to the U.S. Census Department—but that number is growing.

Many American men embrace the idea of job flexibility in order to achieve a better work-life balance with their families. Some men telecommute from home. Others work part-time; sometimes their wife works part-time as well. Many dads are demanding flexible schedules from their employers to accommodate their children's activities and to volunteer in sport leagues, scout troops, etc. Life isn't all about work, and both women and men are seeking flexible work opportunities in order to have more time with their families. And, in most families, a mom would not be able to stay home without the financial support and emotional backing from her spouse. We are all in this together, and while this book is written primarily for women, work-life balance is important to all of us. Our families are our #1 priority.

ACKNOWLEDGMENTS

I would like to thank Kathleen Hughes, publisher at Capital Books, for giving me the wonderful opportunity to write this book. Thanks to Amy Fries for being an outstanding editor.

I would also like to thank all of the moms who shared their inspiring work-life stories for this book, including: Lisa Akers, Diane Anderson, Dr. Tina Bennett, Jane Braumann, Amy Cropper, Victoria Dipalo, Lori Ermi, Teresa Evans-Hunter, Suzan French, Kathy Garino, Meghan Gosk, Debra Haas, Jill Houk, Jennifer Houghton, Brenda Leslie, Amy Long, Jennifer Mangum, Beth Mansfield, Suzan Meredith, Anna Millar, Nadine Monaco, Judy Pettersen, Laura Izon Powell, Marie Risser, Lillian Zarreli Ryals, Elizabeth Ruben, Dr. Jennifer Shu, Melody Spier, Cheryl Stein, Kelly Stettner, Lisa Svendsen, Teresa Todd, Elizabeth Dalton Tyrell, Kerri Westburg, Blair Wilson, Beckye Young, and Dorit Zeevi-Farrington.

Thanks to the following career experts I interviewed for this book: Stacy Blackman, Kyra Cavanaugh, Kellyanne Conway, Shannon Davis, Nicole Belson Goluboff, Gil Gordon, Deborah Epstein Henry, Tory Johnson, Allison O'Kelly, Maryann Perrin, Leslie Spencer Pyle, Anne Ruddy, Liz Pulliam Weston, Chuck Wilsker, and Kathleen Wu.

And, most of all, I would like to acknowledge and express my heartfelt thanks and appreciation to my wonderful family.

—SRA

Disclaimers

The information in this book represents the opinion of the author and is to be used for informational purposes only. Job seekers are encouraged to consult with a career professional since everyone's career situation is different. Neither the author nor publisher are responsible for, or have any liability for, results incurred by readers who follow the advice given in this book.

As of publication, all of the websites included in this book were active. But since websites come and go, some of the links may be inactive by the time you read this book. Please be aware that neither the author nor the publisher is endorsing any of the websites or content on the sites in this book. Please check all websites out carefully before using their services. The included websites are merely a sampling of organizations focused on a particular topic—in most cases there are other similar organizations and websites. If you are affiliated with or aware of an organization that you want us to know about, e-mail the author at author@allmomswork.com for possible inclusion on the book's website.

INTRODUCTION

Should You Stay Home?

"The future belongs to those who believe in the beauty of
their dreams."
> —ELEANOR ROOSEVELT, FORMER FIRST LADY OF
> THE UNITED STATES (1884–1962)

Should you become a stay-at-home mother by joining the
whopping crowd of 5.6 million stay-at-home mothers in
America? It's a big decision. In our hearts, many of us want to
stay home to spend quality and quantity time with our children.
But in our pocketbooks, well . . . ouch! Some experts say
typical stay-at-home mothers give up $1 million in income and
benefits. And staying at home can devastate a woman's career.
Recent studies have found that it's generally very difficult, if
not impossible, to get back into the professional workforce after
being home for a number of years. Depressing, yes, but that's
the reality. So what should you do?

Legions of American women are leaving work to become
stay-at-home moms and finding out-of-box ways to make money
while continuing on their career trajectories from home. These
stay-at-home moms can be more correctly termed as "stay-at-
home *career* moms" because they are continuing their careers on
their own terms, whether working part-time, telecommuting,

or starting a business. These experiences keep their resumes up-to-date and allow them to shape their own work experiences and manage their own time. Many of these women will later decide to re-enter the full-time professional workforce. With careful planning, they should be able to jump right back in where they left off.

This book is divided into three parts. Part One focuses on both long- and short-term strategies for stay-at-home mom career success. Strategies include the ABCs of networking, volunteering, and the importance of keeping in touch with your former employer. Part Two focuses on work options for stay-at-home career moms, and Part Three focuses on making the transition to part-time or full-time employment. Stay-at-home career moms should read these chapters—even if they are planning to stay home for the foreseeable future—as a part of their long-term career strategy.

Important factors for transitioning back into the workforce include:

- Re-igniting your network
- Self-assessment: What do you want to do?
- Do you need a career coach?
- Is it time for a career change?
- Re-inventing yourself
- What is your brand?

In the final two chapters, I address resumes and cover letters, creating your own website, and how to ace your interview. Here is the clincher: *hold your head high and don't apologize*. You should be proud that you stayed home with your children. Your future employer will be impressed by what you have accomplished at home professionally.

Throughout your career, remember: flexibility is the key to long-term success. By reading this book, you will be able to look at your overall career as a series of moves, choices, and scenarios. Remember the kids "Hokey Pokey" song: "You put one foot in, you put one foot out and shake it all about . . . "

Over the next eighteen or so years, you might care for your children exclusively, work part-time, work full time with flexible hours, start a business, telecommute, volunteer, and more. Hey, nothing ever worth it is easy. But for most of us, that's okay. We get to spend quality and quantity time with our children and build our careers at the same time. It is the perfect work-life solution.

PART I

KEEP YOUR EYE ON THE HORIZON:
LONG-RANGE CAREER STRATEGIZING

1 WITH A DOSE OF CREATIVITY, YOU CAN HAVE IT ALL

"Life is not easy for any of us. But what of that? We must have perseverance and above all confidence in ourselves. We must believe that we are gifted for something and that this thing must be attained."
— MARIE CURIE, PHYSICIST (1867–1934)

We have all read the headlines: mommy wars, stay-at-home versus stay-at-work mothers, latchkey children, ruined careers, dirty daycare centers, glass ceilings, nanny cams, and more. It's enough to boggle the mind of any new parent. One of the biggest decisions professional mothers and mothers-to-be have to make is whether and how to continue their career after the birth of their child and future children. While the media would lead us to believe that it is an *either-or* decision—i.e., *either* keep your professional full-time job *or* stay at home full time and raise your children—you don't have to make either choice. The stay-at-work versus stay-at-home divide is a myth. There is a better way—the perfect work-life solution: become a "stay-at-home *career* mom" and raise your children while pursuing employment as a part-time professional or telecommuter, or become an entrepreneur by starting your own business.

In a 2007 Pew Research Center study, 60 percent of working mothers said that working part-time outside the home would be the ideal. That's up from 48 percent in 1997. Only 21 percent of working mothers said a full-time job would be the ideal, down from 32 percent in 1997. More than one in four employed women work part-time, according to a government study.

Meanwhile, legions of mothers are creating lucrative home-based entrepreneurial businesses. Starting a home-based business allows mothers to exercise their creativity and their educational and professional background without sacrificing their family life and paying for daycare. These entrepreneurial women—Baby Boomers and Generation X and Y alike—are not satisfied with staying home just "baking cookies." If they are baking cookies consistently, they're probably also marketing their recipe to a high-priced wholesaler and maybe even publishing their own cookbook.

Telecommuting is also on the rise. Internet technology has enabled millions of people to work from home, a trend that will continue to skyrocket in the future. Today, more than 15 percent of women work at home at least once per week as part of their main job, according to the latest government statistics.

Access to technology—from the Internet to faxes and cell phones—makes home business or telecommuting a viable reality. It's a boom time—the perfect time to become a stay-at-home career mom.

Women today want the flexibility to manage their own schedules. In the 1980s, many professional women worked full time in powerhouse careers. It was the era of trying to break the glass ceiling for career advancement while working fifty, sixty, or more hours a week. It was a great era for women's professional advancement, but many women felt their family lives suffered and that their children, termed by some as "latchkey" children, grew up spending much of their time without supervision or in daycare.

The 1990s, the age of the so-called "soccer moms," was in some ways a throwback to earlier eras. Tired of balancing their time and not spending both quality and quantity time with their children, many women quit, or at least wanted to quit, to become full-time stay-at-home moms. Now we're undergoing a new major trend, a hybrid of the trends of the 1980s and 1990s— women are finding creative ways to manage their own time by becoming stay-at-home career moms as part-time employees, telecommuters, or home-business owners.

Should you stay home or go back after the birth of your child? Ignore the media and decide what's right for you and your family. The "mommy wars" myth is based on media frenzy and hype. Suburban moms are not at each other's throats over their decisions to continue to work after they have children or stay home. In the real world, moms of all stripes help each other out. Yes, there are some highly vocal partisans on both sides, but they are in the minority. Some of them argue that you have to work full time in order to keep pace with the women's movement and that work is the only path to personal fulfillment. Critics on the other side say that you need to stay home full time in order to be a good mother. By and large, however, the vast majority of moms are not concerned about everyone else—they just want what's best for themselves and their family. Don't you?

Some experts warn about the economic costs and risks of staying home—and they are right. By being a stay-at-home career mom, you will keep focused on your career plan and will always be ready to jump back in, if necessary. If you find yourself unexpectedly divorced or widowed, or if your partner loses his job or becomes disabled, you will be in a good position to get back into the workforce. As a stay-at-home career mom, you will have maintained your professional skills and network. There are no guarantees in life. A stay-at-work mom may become unexpectedly laid off down the road and have a difficult time finding another suitable job.

The aim of this book is not to disparage full-time working moms. Many women find that working full time is the ideal choice and/or the only way they can afford to raise their family. Legions of women work full time, and many find creative ways to try to obtain the flexibility that they need and desire. Flexible work options will be discussed in Chapter Seven.

Some pundits have dubbed flexible work options as "mommy track" careers, as if these types of career setups are somehow inferior to working fifty or more hours a week and having little time with your family. On the contrary, flexible work options allow you to carve out your own life, in the manner that *you* desire. You can make it work, whether going back to work and finding quality childcare or staying home for several months or many years. Either option is viable, but involves careful planning and important considerations.

Women's career concerns are the focus of this book. While a growing number of men are choosing to stay home at some point in their careers, men tend to have different issues and concerns. That said, many of these career strategies are equally beneficial for both stay-at-home career moms and dads.

Career planning is critical to long-term career success. Here is the hard, cold reality: it's not advisable to just quit your job and blindly hope to re-enter the professional job market two, five, or twenty years later. Chances are that you will be back at entry-level or not find a suitable job at all. Unless you are lucky, you may be literally throwing your education and work experience away. Instead, you need a plan and a strategy that you will invoke from Day One off the job.

Stay-at-home career moms have an important advantage in today's job market. It is rare these days for a person to work at one company from graduation to retirement. Employees today are more like "free agents" who job hop strategically and work for a number of companies over the course of their career. It's not unusual to change the entire focus of a career five to six times over the course of a professional lifetime. In today's fluid job market, a stay-at-home career mom can strategize their career and be able to later jump right back on the career carousel to their next job.

For all the moms who choose to work full time or stay-at-home full time exclusively, three cheers, both options are possible and can be workable and professionally and personally satisfying. But for those of us who want it all, being a stay-at-home career mom is the best way to balance our family priorities and professional goals. Being a stay-at-home career mom is not about finding any job and punching a time clock for the next twenty, thirty, or forty years. It's about creating your own opportunities. It takes ingenuity, creativity, and spunk. Hey, you've got all that, right? If so, read on, and best of luck with your career and your children. This is the best time of your life.

Keep Your Eye on the Horizon: Long-Term Strategies

Stay-at-home career moms need to create a long-term strategy to maintain their professional platform and prepare for possible re-entry into the full-time workforce. Keep in mind that some moms will decide to never go back to work. They will launch successful businesses or find working part-time to be a professionally viable solution. That said, it's important to keep all options open. Being a successful stay-at-home career mom is about having *options*. With careful planning, a stay-at-home career mom can have it *all*—time to spend with their children at home and short-term and long-range career success.

Long-term strategies for success include formulating an effective exit strategy, continuing to build your professional network, and volunteering strategically. By using these strategies, you will keep your options open for possible re-entry into the professional workforce, whether in two years or twenty.

Parting Is Such Sweet Sorrow

Your stay-at-home career strategizing should start before quitting your job. Whether you love, hate, or are lukewarm about your job, it's important to part on good terms. This is your last reference, and you may need them some day. So, tempting as it may be, if it happens that you don't like your current job, don't go running out the door like you won the multimillion-dollar jackpot lottery. You need to plan an exit strategy. If you're pregnant, let your boss know as soon as you start to show. Come up with a viable plan that works for both of you. Are you planning to come back to work full time after the baby is born? Do you prefer to work part-time? Can you telecommute?

But what if you plan to come back and then change your mind? It's an all too common scenario—it happened to me. You see your baby for the first time and just can't go back to work. If you can afford it, and it works for your family, then contact your boss and be honest. Explain your change of heart. Offer to do whatever it takes to find and train your replacement.

If you decide to leave your company but want to keep your affiliation with it, consider negotiating the possibility of continuing to work for your company on a consulting basis or as a freelancer. Identify possible freelance or occasional work that you can do for your company. Depending on your skills and your company's size, you might consider offering to do an array of different tasks. For example, you might propose to update the company's annual report, write or edit a company newsletter, or organize the annual holiday party. There are myriad possibilities. Try to identify where there is a need and offer to fill it.

So Long, but Don't Forget Me

It's important to stay in touch with your former employer and contacts at your old workplace. While it may be tempting to just drop off the professional horizon, stay-at-home career moms need to keep their contacts current. Between diaper changes or runs to soccer practice, make sure that you stay in touch with your former employer. How? Keep in e-mail contact with your former bosses and colleagues, whether they remain in the same organization or move on to another company. While it may be easy to send informal e-mails to colleagues who are friends, it pays to be creative and find ways to keep in touch with all of your contacts.

Examples of good reasons to e-mail former bosses and colleagues:

- To congratulate them on an accomplishment—for example, a promotion or job change.
- To pass along a news item that may be of interest to them. Include a brief note on your take on the news article and

why you sent it: "I thought this might be of interest to you . . ." But don't send an article that you know they would have obviously seen—for example, an article in the area newspaper that everyone reads. (Don't forward jokes or junk e-mails.)

- To mention your accomplishments as a volunteer or in a part-time job that is analogous to functions of your former job.
- To send holiday wishes. This is where you can put the cutesy pictures of your kids.

Networking Is the Magic Key

What if you have absolutely no intention of working for this company again or plan to stay-at-home for twenty years, switch careers, or start your own business? Or what if you are too busy with the daily responsibilities of raising your children? Do it anyway! At least send a yearly holiday card. Why? Because networking is the *magic key* to career success.

Keeping in touch with your former employer is one part of a stay-at-home career mom's networking strategy. Networking is critical so you don't lose your former identity as a career professional.

Ideally, you should keep and expand your network of career contacts from Day One of leaving a job. It's never too late, however. Stay-at-home career moms can re-ignite a career network at any time.

Your Thirty-Second Commercial

Stay-at-home career moms need to develop a thirty-second commercial, which is essentially a brief statement of who you are, where you've been, and where you are going. For example, "I am Jane Doe, I worked as a marketing manager at XYZ publishing for ten years. I am presently a stay-at-home career mom. Right now I am working on several consulting projects. I plan to re-enter the workforce in marketing, but I hope to transfer my skills as a marketer to the IT field."

You will use your thirty-second commercial often while networking, so think carefully about what you want to say. It's important to rehearse your commercial. Try to sound positive, enthusiastic, and natural, in other words—try to sound like what you are saying was not rehearsed. It's a tall order and takes a lot of practice.

It's vital to project confidence when making your thirty-second commercial. By making this pitch, you will show the other person that you're self-assured in terms of your career and your decision to stay home. Project the message that you have no doubts about your professional competence and ability to re-enter the workforce at a future date of your own choosing. Confidence is your best defense to any naysayer you may encounter who erroneously believes that you can't "have it all."

As a stay-at-home career mom, you have the advantage of being able to network without having the pressure of needing to find a job right away. Since you're not looking for a job immediately, you can feel more relaxed when meeting new people. This will pay off in the long term when you start looking for a job and already have a network of contacts that you have diligently cultivated.

While networking, focus on building rapport and communicating your 30-second commercial with confidence. Ask appropriate questions. Be yourself and let your personality shine. You will meet people, have fun, and build your network for future career success.

Critical Strategy: Association Membership

Stay-at-home career moms are advised to join or maintain their memberships with professional associations and organizations in their industry. Membership in professional associations shows your peers and prospective employers that you are serious about your career. It's a great place to network and meet people in your field, and you'll gain knowledge about developments in your industry.

It's advisable to get a sitter and go to professional meetings or conferences when possible while you're raising your children.

Collect business cards and use your e-mail strategy to keep in touch, if appropriate and relevant. Let your new contacts know that you're a stay-at-home career mom and have temporarily stepped out of the full-time workforce. Most people will get it. If they don't, move on and network with another contact. You'll find people who share your values.

You can find professional organizations and associations online by accessing "Weddles Association Directory": Weddles. com/associations.

Another good site for links to networking organizations is: Job-Hunt.org (click on "Associations and Societies"). A similar database, "Associations Unlimited," is available at most public libraries. Another popular resource is *The Encyclopedia of Associations*, a book published by Thomson Gale, found in the reference section of many libraries.

You can also find associations by using Google or another search engine and entering keywords like "association" or "organization" and industry keywords, for example, "banking" or "nursing." Google, MSN, and Yahoo all maintain lists of professional associations. Better yet, use this as an opportunity to network by sending an e-mail to some of your former colleagues, asking for suggestions on good organizations to join.

Keep up-to-date with industry developments. Read professional journals and websites. Post an occasional comment with your name on online industry sites. Your name may end up linked to the comment on Google, which is impressive when future potential employers do a pre-employment search on your name.

Online Networking: The New Frontier

Online networking is an excellent way for stay-at-home career moms to make contacts. A number of business-related networking websites—including LinkedIn.com, Ryze.com, and Spoke.com—enable users to post professional information and network with other members. There are also industry-specific online networking sites, including, for example, MediaBistro. com (for media/journalism networking) and the Project Management Institute, PMI.org. You may want to post your professional information on one of these sites. It may lead to short-term consulting opportunities and the opportunity to network with others in your industry.

Online business networks work like their social networking counterparts, MySpace.com, for example. On networking sites, you post your profile and then invite other professionals you know to join your network. As your network expands, you increase your connections. You can find new connections by searching for your former colleagues and classmates, for example, to see if they are presently participating on that network.

Participation in an online network may be useful down the road if you decide to pursue part-time or full-time employment. Through these sites, you can network with others in a company, industry, or geographical area. You can find people who worked with you previously or went to your university. Most of these sites are presently free, but offer optional paid service upgrades. Many companies now search for job candidates through these sites.

Build Connections via Blogging

If you have the time and skills, you may want to start a web log, or "blog" about some aspect of your career field. A blog

Birds of a Feather

Check out MeetUp.com to find other people who share your interests in many cities nationwide. There are hundreds of career groups, parenting groups, stay-at-home mom groups, and many more hobby and interest-specific groups. You can start your own group in your area via this website.

is an online journal that you update frequently. Free hosting is available through such sites as Blogger.com and WordPress. com. It's important to write a professional blog that's free of typos and grammatical errors. Consider including short video clips or a podcast (audio clip) on your blog. Spend some time on it. You may get more Internet traffic than you ever imagined. By writing a blog, potential future employers will have concrete evidence of your continuing interest and knowledge of your career field. You can provide links to other blogs and websites, which may lead to your blog being linked by others. Many people have become well known in their industry by creating successful blogs.

About Town: Networking through Civic Organizations

Membership in civic, political, community, and religious organizations is another excellent way to expand your professional network. You'll meet other professionals and feel good about making a difference in your community. Some organizations will allow family participation in their activities. While these types of organizations will not be directly relevant to your career field, one fringe benefit of your participation is that you will build your personal network by meeting other people in many industries. Some of the people may work in areas that are somehow connected to yours, for example, as a supplier or competitor.

Military Networking

Veterans should check out the career section of Military.com. Click on "Career Network" to find veterans who are willing to help current and future job seekers. There is also a military spouse career center on the site.

But I Left My College Years Ago

Networking opportunities are available through the alumni network at your former college or university. Contact the alumni office via your university's webpage. There are usually multiple opportunities to network with other graduates in your career field. Oftentimes there is an online directory of graduates who are willing to talk to other graduates about careers in their field. Some universities maintain an online social and business-networking site for their graduates.

If you can swing it, go to some alumni gatherings so that you can network with other grads in person. There are sometimes smaller alumni groups for residents of different cities nationwide who meet for informal networking sessions. If you haven't already, ask to be included on the alumni mailing list. You will likely receive a newsletter or magazine with news about other graduates and their career accomplishments.

If you belonged to an honorary society or a sorority, be sure to check their websites. Many of these organizations have extensive networking opportunities for their members.

Check out sites such as Classmates.com to find your former high school, college, and military friends.

Corporate Alumni Organizations

Some companies have alumni organizations for their former employees, a positive sign that these companies value the idea of maintaining contact with previous staff. Check out your former company's webpage to see if they have an alumni club. Alumni organizations can be accessed via sites such as CorporateAlumni.net, Alumni.net, and Job-Hunt.org (click on "Company, Military, and Government Alumni Networks").

Don't Forget the Playground

You can also network in your own community. As a mother, you will meet people at playgrounds, swim meets, ballet practice, and more. Many times it will seem like mom-to-mom conversations are limited to diaper brands or home decorating. It does not have to be that way, however. Ask moms what they did or are doing professionally. You may have more in common than you think. These people may be your future references or let you know about job opportunities one day. Sometimes their husbands or friends may be your future link to career opportunities.

Family and neighbors are also part of your personal network. If possible, keep them updated with your career endeavors. Remember, they are your biggest cheerleaders.

Your network can also include the professionals that you interact with regularly, for example, your doctor, realtor, lawyer, insurance agent, etc. Service people, such as your drycleaner, painter, contractor, etc., may also be valuable contacts. They may not know of jobs or consulting opportunities for you, but they may be able to connect you to someone who does.

Keep in mind that you don't want to network with people outside of your close business network (people in your industry) solely with the intention of trying to advance your career. If you have a suitable opportunity, however, it doesn't hurt to use your thirty-second commercial and see if they offer to assist you or introduce you to their contacts.

You never know who has a friend or a friend of a friend . . .

Women's Networking Groups

In many areas of the country, women have started women's networking groups to help them meet other women in the same type of career mode. As a stay-at-home career mom, you may want to join or start this type of networking group. Find existing women's networking groups by entering "women's networking group" and your city, into a Google search. Other listings may be posted in your local newspaper or on your local library's bulletin board.

There are many national and international women's business networking groups. Some are general in focus and others are specific to an industry. Examples of industry specific women's organizations include the American Association of University Women, AAUW.org, and the Association for Women in Computing, AWC-HQ.org.

Starting a Support/Play Group

Some stay-at-home moms have joined or started their own support groups. Typically, a group of moms will get together on a regular basis and talk about their short-term and long-range

A Sampling of Women's Networking Organizations

- American Business Women's Association, ABWA. org, networking group for women in diverse occupations.
- Business and Professional Women USA, BPWUSA. org, organization focused on issues related to equity, job advancement, and networking.
- DowntownWomensClub.com, sponsors women's networking activities at a number of cities nationwide.
- Forté Foundation, ForteFoundation.org, a consortium of major corporations and top business schools, offers career advice and networking opportunities for women.
- National Association of Female Executives, Nafe. com, is a businesswomen's association with more than 125,000 members.
- WomenAtWorkNetwork.com, a network of current and returning professional women seeking work-life balance.

career goals while their children play together. Find existing groups through your local newspaper or on the library bulletin board. Sometimes you will make lasting friendships while keeping focused on your short-term and long-range career goals.

Volunteering—Make a Difference while Advancing Your Career

While you will be incredibly busy as a new mom, keep your eye on the horizon. It's important to try to carve out some time in your busy schedule to volunteer. Volunteering is a great way

Salary Equivalents for Stay-at-Home Moms

Did you ever wonder what it would cost to pay outsiders to do all the tasks a stay-at-home mom is typically responsible for each day? According to Salary.com, a stay-at-home mom's salary in 2008 should be $116,805. Stay-at-home moms typically do the work of ten jobs each day: housekeeper, daycare center teacher, cook, computer operator, laundry-machine operator, janitor, facilities manager, van driver, CEO, and psychologist. According to the Salary.com survey, stay-at-home moms typically work a ninety-two-hour workweek.

A full-time working mom's "at-home" salary was calculated at $68,405 in 2008, in addition to the salary they earn in the workplace, according to Salary.com.

to meet people and expand your network and use, update, or learn new skills. It keeps your resume current.

By the time your children get to preschool you will probably be inundated with requests to volunteer, so choose your opportunities wisely. While you may want to do some volunteering for the fun of it, also take on some responsibility that will both "make a difference" and advance your career. Keep in mind that many women choose to stay home in the first place so that they can be room mom, field-trip chaperone, etc. These opportunities are fun, memorable, and allow you to spend quality time with your child—so by all means, do not forgo these opportunities just to take on professionally oriented volunteer positions. Try to balance your time volunteering as a room mom with volunteering opportunities that use your professional skills. For example, if you're a finance professional, you may want to volunteer to work as treasurer for the school's Parent Teacher Organization (PTO) or Girl Scouts. If a volunteer opportunity reinforces your current skill set or gives you the opportunity to learn new skills, then go for it.

Enthusiasm is the key to having a memorable and enjoyable volunteer experience. Down the line, someone may recommend you for a job or agree to be a reference on the basis of your performance as a volunteer. Make sure your heart is in it, however—no organization wants a volunteer that is not dedicated to their cause or is volunteering solely for their own personal gain.

Volunteering opportunities are available at local, regional, national, and international organizations. The Federal Government maintains a massive online clearinghouse of volunteering opportunities at USAFreedomCorps.gov. You can use this site by entering your zip code and the volunteer category that is of interest to you. Volunteer categories on this site include:

- Animals and Environment
- Arts and Culture
- Children and Youth
- Civic and Community
- Education and Tech
- Faith-based Organizations
- Health and Human Services
- Public Safety

Stay-at-home career moms may want to check on virtual volunteering opportunities that are available through the site. As a virtual volunteer, you will work at home from your home computer. Examples of virtual volunteering opportunities include grant writing, accounting, tutoring, or computer programming. You will have the opportunity to update your resume, use your professional skills, and make contacts without leaving the house. The disadvantage is that you will not be

Organizations with Volunteer Opportunities

The following is a sampling of organizations that feature volunteer opportunities:

- AmeriCorps: AmeriCorps.org, is a network of local, state, and national service programs that connects Americans each year to volunteering activities related to education, public safety, health, and the environment.
- Habitat for Humanity International: Habitat.org. Volunteers build houses for needy or homeless families.
- Idealist.org: Volunteer-opportunity listings across the nation and worldwide.
- United National Volunteers: OnlineVolunteering. org. Volunteers work virtually from their home computer on sustainable development activities.
- United Way of America: Unitedway.org. Volunteer opportunities in community-based organizations.
- Volunteer Match: VolunteerMatch.org, nonprofit Internet recruiting clearinghouse for more than 40,000 organizations.

networking in person, but this may be the best short-term setup for new moms.

You can also volunteer as a family by accessing relevant opportunities on this site. This is a great way to teach your children the value of helping others and to spend quality together as a family.

Volunteering at Associations

While staying at home, you may want to volunteer to work on

a committee for a professional association. For example, you might consider working on a public relations or membership committee. Through your participation, you'll meet new people, interact with others in the organization, and get your name out there—possibly on a list of volunteers in the association newsletter. Generally speaking, you won't have to make a big time commitment for these types of volunteer positions. Most of the other volunteers will be employed full time, and like you, will have a limited amount of time to spare for volunteering.

You may also want to volunteer at an association conference. By spending a few hours at the check-in table or passing out brochures, for example, you will have the opportunity to meet industry leaders and future colleagues.

Consider volunteering as a member of a panel discussion if you're up-to-date on industry developments and have maintained your expertise. This type of exposure will maintain and enhance your professional visibility. If you're still current with industry developments and can set up a speaking engagement, then go for it. The rewards will be immeasurable for your career. Speaking engagements need not be limited to professional conferences. You can also volunteer to make industry-related presentations at local community colleges or other venues. Are you interested in teaching? Consider teaching an adult education class in your community related to your industry.

Another way to keep yourself known is to write freelance articles for online and offline association and general-industry publications. Check out the website for an industry publication. Click on "writer's guidelines" or "article submission guidelines." The requirements will be spelled out. You can also write industry-related articles for your local or regional newspaper.

But I'm Too Busy!

By volunteering and networking, you make contacts and "keep your feet in the game." Any of these ideas will be knock-out entries to your resume. But where do you find the time? You will be incredibly busy with your child or children. If you have a newborn, you may have to put off all of it for now. But stay-at-home career moms should try to do some of these resume builders at different times in the coming months and years. Make a plan and see what works for you. Be flexible. You will need to tweak your plan often. You will have more time when your kids get older.

Moms with newborns may want to consider virtual volunteering and virtual networking. As your children get older, you can set up play dates for your kids, get sitters, and consider enrolling them in a "Mom's Morning Out" program. These programs are generally "pre" preschools and allow moms some free time, often a morning or two per week. Or you could pair up with another mom and take turns watching each other's kids one day a week each. It will give you both some needed work time and your kids more time to play with friends. Before you know it, your kids will be in preschool and then elementary school. You will drop them off at the bus stop with the bittersweet mixed emotions of relief at having time to pursue your at home career and the sadness of missing them all day.

It's critical to encourage your husband or partner to share with household responsibilities and childcare. Here is where we have a big advantage over the previous generation. Men today are more likely to shoulder more responsibility for housework and raising their children. But, in many families, women still do the majority of household and childcare responsibilities, according to Catalyst, a NY-based business research organization.

Some stay-at-home career moms actually decide to stay home partially so as to prevent the exhaustion of working "the second shift," i.e., working all day outside the home and then coming home to do chores full time at home. It's important to carefully negotiate the division of household chores and childcare with your partner.

Here's an important tip for both parents: focus on trying to stay organized. While this may seem like an insurmountable challenge, try to organize your household to the best degree possible. For example, set up a schedule for housework, shopping, and errands. Establish a bedtime for your children. Organize the house so there is a place to store toys, books, and so on. As your children get older, teach them to pitch in and do some chores.

Remember that being a stay-at-home career mom means balancing your priorities on a daily basis. As such, you are your own manager and can make a flexible plan. Your baby took an unexpected nap? Great, head for the computer (tip: not the vacuum cleaner, *please*). Your child has a play date next door? Okay, write an entry for your blog. Easy? Of course not! But for a stay-at-home career mom flexibility is essential. The extra efforts that you make will pay off and are critical to your longer-term career strategy. By taking the time to plan your career by networking and volunteering, you will lay the foundation to re-enter your career at a future date of your own choice.

2 CONTINUING ED 101

"Learning is not attained by chance, it must be sought for
with ardor and attended to with diligence."
—ABIGAIL ADAMS, FORMER FIRST LADY OF
THE UNITED STATES (1744–1818)

Whether you dream of getting your BA or PhD, MA, MBA,
or law degree—now may be the perfect time to continue
your education. Other options include taking continuing education courses, courses toward a certificate program, or other
types of short-term training.

Returning to college can be very challenging for a mom
with a young child or children. You will need to balance caring
for your children and family with going to classes, writing
research papers, and doing homework. On the other hand, if you
wait until you're back at work to return to school, then you'll
have even less time. Chances are that you'll never go back to
school at all. Many moms opt to return to college and take day
classes when their youngest child starts going to school. Others
decide to start classes sooner and either attend classes at night
while their spouse is at home or use daycare.

Even if you're not planning to return to college, you may
need to take courses during your years at home. If you're a

teacher or lawyer, or in some other profession that requires certification or licensure, then you may need to take courses to maintain your status while staying at home. It's advisable to take your courses now rather than waiting until re-entry, when you're trying to balance work and family. Inexpensive courses may be found via local colleges and/or through distance learning. Consult the licensing agency for your profession.

Don't Be a Techno Rip Van Winkle
Keeping up with technology is critical. You may need to take courses or self-study to keep abreast with the rapidly evolving changes. At a minimum, as of this writing, a stay-at-home career mom needs to be proficient with Internet searching, e-mail, Microsoft Word, PowerPoint, and Excel. But this may change any day . . . so pay attention to any technology changes that affect your field.

Reasons to consider returning to college include the opportunity to interact with adults. As a student, you'll be able to network with instructors and classmates. By getting your degree, you'll set a good example for your children about the importance and value of education. Your children will be there when you toss your cap at graduation—a lifelong memory for the both of you.

If you're thinking that it's too late, erase that thought from your mind. More than 30 percent of today's college students are adult learners, according to the Lumina Foundation in Education. Millions of other adults take online courses. If you're wondering about the advisability of returning to college at thirty, forty, or fifty years old, remember that the time will pass anyway. Why not make it productive and use that time to get your degree?

Initial Factors to Consider
Whether you're considering an undergraduate or a graduate degree, or just taking a few courses, there are several common factors that everyone needs to consider:

•   How will you pay for it?

- Is a campus "family friendly"?
- Balancing studying and parenting
- Finding the right campus
- Pros and cons of distance learning

How Will You Pay for It?

One of the critical factors is how to pay for the tuition and related costs. While you may be able to afford the costs of continuing education courses or short-term training, you may need financial help, in the form of loans, grants, or scholarships, to pay for the costs of attending a degree program. Financial aid is widely available to adult students in degree programs and is not always tied to financial need. If you're interested in pursing a degree, you will need to find out how much it will cost and what types of financial aid and scholarships may be available.

As an adult student, your family may be eligible for certain tax benefits. For details, consult the Internal Revenue Service, IRS.gov. Benefits and deductions are explained in the IRS bulletin #970 "Tax Benefits for Education."

Contact colleges and universities directly to find out about additional funding sources, scholarships, assistantships/ fellowships, and grants for which you may qualify. As a stay-at-home career mom, you will probably start slowly and take courses on a part-time basis, which will affect the types of scholarships and aid that will be available. If you can swing a full-time schedule, then you may receive more funding. On the other hand, if you're only taking a few courses at a time, then you may be able to afford the hourly tuition rates.

For information on financial aid and scholarships, start by visiting:

- Back2College.com, a site focused on adult education, click on "Financial Aid"
- Career One Stop: ACINET.org, click on "Education and Training" and then "Financial Aid" or "Scholarships"
- The College Board: CollegeBoard.com, click on "For

Students" and then "Pay for College." This site also includes a scholarship search.

- Petersons.com, click on "Pay for School" to find relevant articles and a scholarship search.
- Princeton Review Scholarship Search: PrincetonReview. com, click on "Scholarships and Aid" and "Search for Scholarships"
- Sallie Mae: SallieMae.com, click on "Finding Free Money," "Finding Ways to Pay," and "College Answer," a scholarship search.

Is a Campus "Family Friendly"?

For many moms, their decision on going back to college will depend on how to balance parenting and taking their classes. It's critical that a campus is "family friendly."

The good news is that most colleges have multiple services to accommodate adult learners with families.

As an adult learner, you may prefer to attend a college that offers:

- Advising and support for adult students
- Affordable on-site childcare
- Distance-learning options
- Fast-track options and credit for life/work experiences
- Flexible scheduling, whether during the day, in the evenings, and/or on weekends.

Balancing Studying and Parenting

As a stay-at-home career mom, your biggest challenge will be balancing your time between studying and parenting, not to mention finding time for your spouse, to exercise, volunteer, do some housework, and everything else. To be a successful student, you'll need to multitask effectively and study whenever possible. Start slowly. Take one or two courses and add more if it works for you. If your children are older, study alongside them while they do their homework. You'll be their greatest inspiration. Yes, it will be difficult to fit it all in. But you can. With careful planning and organization, you can achieve an optimal studying-parenting balance that works for you and your family.

FINDING THE RIGHT CAMPUS

Your choice of colleges will likely depend on what's in your region. If you're lucky, there will be at least one suitable college within reasonable commuting distance. Otherwise, you may want to consider distance-learning options.

To start researching area colleges, access sites such as:

- College Board: CollegeBoard.com
- Peterson's: Petersons.com
- *U.S. News and World Report*'s "America's Best Colleges": USnews.com/usnews/edu/college/tools/search.php

On these sites you can find detailed information on prospective area colleges, including academic programs offered, cost, admission requirements, selectivity, programs and services, and more.

The *U.S. News & World Report* site focuses on college rankings, which is a controversial practice, but nevertheless a factor that you should take into consideration. It may or may not be important to you and your career if you attend a "prestige" college. Here you will need to carefully research and consider if this is an important factor in terms of your long-term career goals. If you're planning to become a teacher, for example, a state college may be the best bet in terms of financial cost versus expected salary. On the other hand, if you're planning a career in investment banking, then you may want to consider attending the "most prestigious" regionally located college in your field.

PROS AND CONS OF DISTANCE LEARNING

As a stay-at-home career mom, you may prefer to take all or some of your classes online. Many accredited colleges now offer

In a Mom's Own Words
Suzan French: A Mom Who Returned to College to Get a Business Degree

Suzan French, an Allentown, Pennsylvania, mom was able to make the jump from an administrative job to an executive-level position by going back to college. Just getting to the college was an ongoing challenge—French commuted sixty miles each way from her Allentown home to Philadelphia.

"My daughters were three and ten years old when I decided it was time for me to go back to school and complete my degree. I was a single mother, working in a job that kept me away from them for too long and for too little money. I wanted better for them, for us. A friend encouraged me to apply to Wharton's undergraduate program at the University of Pennsylvania. I applied, was accepted, and over the next two years completed dual degrees in Marketing (from Wharton) and Communications (from Annenberg) via an intense schedule of day and evening classes. I had been working in public relations prior to returning to school, but only on an administrative level. After obtaining my degree, I was able to secure a senior-level position, and today I run my own business.

"Balancing it all was never easy, but it got easier as I learned to streamline. For instance, I'd cook a week's worth of meals on weekends; and I became a better student, not procrastinating because the time I had for schoolwork was so limited. Still, most nights I got very little sleep. Driving me the whole time, however, was my children. I wanted a better life for them. They deserved it, and I was the only one who was going to give it to them. It was the strongest motivator . . . Graduation day wasn't just for me—it was for all of us."

online courses—and in some cases entire degrees—via distance learning. It may be a good option for you because you will likely not need childcare and may be able to work and study around your child or children's napping or school schedule.

Distance-learning programs are gaining in popularity and acceptance. In many cases, the courses that you will take and your degree will be identical to that taken by a student on-site at a college. Your future employer may respect the extra initiative that distance learning requires.

Is distance learning right for you? To be a successful online learner, you will need to be extremely self-motivated, have excellent time-management skills, be an excellent writer, and have good computer and Internet skills.

As a distance learner, you will miss out on some of the finer points of college life—classroom discussion, presenting in front of an audience, in-person group work, etc., but as a stay-at-home career mom, it may be your best option. You can also opt to take a mixture of online and traditional courses at a college.

To find out about distance-learning programs and courses, access Petersons.com and click on "Online and Continuing Education." You can search for online programs via a school name, your intended field of study, or degree/award level. Distance-learning courses are offered at many private and public colleges and universities nationwide, from community colleges to the Ivy League universities. A number of accredited commercially owned colleges offer courses exclusively or primarily via distance learning.

When assessing distance-learning options, be sure that the college is regionally accredited by the appropriate agency. Unfortunately, some online colleges falsely claim to be accredited when they are actually "diploma mills" where people pay to get a degree. For more information, consult the webpage for the Council for Higher Education Accreditation: CHEA. org. Click on "Databases and Directories" to find accredited institutions and programs, and "CHEA Recognized Accrediting Organization Directory" to check out accrediting agencies. Be sure to click on "Diploma Mills and Accreditation Mills" to find out about scams.

Educational Options to Explore

As a first step toward going back to school, carefully consider your career goals and what degree or courses you will need to obtain it. Depending on your prior education and career goals, there are many options for your continuing education, including enrolling in:

- Community college programs
- Certificate programs
- Vocational & short-term training
- Undergraduate programs
- Graduate & MBA programs
- Law school programs

Continuing Ed for a Career Change

If you're considering a career change or need to upgrade your skills, you may need to seek additional education, whether in the form of another degree or by taking continuing education courses. There are many options, depending on your career goals. Short-term training may be available at a community college or vocational school, or college or university, on a degree or non-degree basis.

Community Colleges

These aren't just for recent high school grads. Whether you have never attended college or you already have an advanced degree, your local community college may offer courses and/or certificate programs to enable you to make a career change or update your professional qualifications. Classes are inexpensive and are usually offered during the day or evening. Distance-learning options are often available.

Certificate programs may include such tracks as dental orthodontic assistant, digital video and filmmaking production, management, computer technology, medical office administration, and many more. Check the website for your local community college system to find out about available certificate program opportunities.

Continuing Education at Four-Year Colleges

Have you dreamed of going to Harvard or Georgetown? You might consider taking continuing education courses at those or at one of hundreds of other colleges and universities nationwide. At most colleges, you can take a range of undergraduate or graduate-level credit or non-credit courses on a continuing education/non-degree basis. Formal admission to a university is usually not required, and you may be able to transfer credit courses taken on a non-degree basis into a degree program later on. Courses may be held during the daytime, in the evenings, or on weekends. Distance-learning, continuing-education opportunities are available through many colleges.

Fast-track professional certificate programs are available at colleges and universities nationwide and via distance learning in a wide array of fields—including everything from financial planning to public relations to project management. To complete the certificate program, you will be required to take a series of credit or non-credit courses. Certificate programs can be a bridge to make a career change to another field. Or, you may want to complete a certificate program to get back up-to-date in your career field if you have been home for a number of years. Admission to the certificate program may be required. Check the websites for your local colleges and universities for more information about available opportunities.

Sampling of Certificate Programs

If you're thinking about a career change, consider completing a certificate program in the career field that you hope to enter. Opportunities vary by university. Here is a sampling of some certificate programs that may be available to launch you into fast-growing career fields.

- Event Planning
- Financial Planning
- Forensic Accounting
- Gerontology
- Human Resources

- Information Technology
- Journalism
- Leadership Coaching
- Museum and Exhibition Design
- Nonprofit Management
- Paralegal
- Public Relations
- Real Estate
- Technical Writing

Vocational and Short-Term Training

If you're eyeing a career in a vocational area, which includes careers such as cosmetology, culinary arts, travel and tourism, landscape design, etc., perhaps with the intent of starting your own business, consider short-term training to learn those skills. Occupations requiring vocational training comprise some of the "fastest growing occupations" in America through 2016, according to the U.S. Bureau of Labor Statistics.

Consult the website for your local government for workforce development and vocational training programs. Links to extensive information on vocational education can be found on the Vocational Information Center website: Khake.com.

Is It Time to Finish Your BA?

If you never attended college or did not finish your degree, now may be the time to start anew. As a stay-at-home career mom, returning to college is an excellent strategy for career success.

Returning to college will give you the credentials necessary to compete for higher-level, better-paying jobs. While many occupations can be classified as "college preferred," the reality is that college grads will be in a better position to be hired for these types of positions and have more promotion opportunities down the line. Without a college degree, you may be stuck in the secretarial pool while dreaming of becoming a manager. And chances are that you will not get promoted into that job— without a college degree.

In today's information-based economy, increasing numbers of jobs are requiring advanced skills, training, and education. Jobs that employ primarily college graduates are projected to be the "fastest growing in the nation," and more than three-quarters of these occupations are expected to grow significantly faster than other types of careers, according to the U.S. Bureau of Labor Statistics.

Many jobs require a BA or advanced or professional degree, especially in large metropolitan areas with a highly educated workforce. Nationwide, one-third of women aged twenty-five through twenty-nine, and 29 percent of both women and men, had a college degree in 2007, according to the U.S. Census Bureau. In some areas, the percentage of the population with college degrees is much higher, including Seattle, San Francisco, Washington, DC, Raleigh, and Boston.

If you're curious about the stats for your area, access factfinder.Census.gov and put the name of your city or county into the search.

But whether you live in a "highly educated" area or not, you can usually count on a bigger paycheck if you have a college degree. According to a 2007 College Board study, those with a BA earn 60 percent more than those with a high school diploma. Over the course of your entire career, you will earn over $800,000 more if you have an undergraduate degree.

Fast-Track Your Undergraduate Degree

Most colleges have an adult-education department and advisors to help you get transfer credit for your prior college coursework and to help you design a fast-track plan for completing your degree.

Some of you may have completed nearly all of the coursework toward your degree already and should, therefore, plan to complete your degree in as few courses as possible. In this case, it's not important to choose a major—just to get your degree completed. Keep in mind that 45 percent of people end up working in different career fields than their declared major, according to recent statistics. Obtaining your degree in philosophy, art history, *whatever*—will enable you to have the liberal arts background necessary to obtain jobs and additional compensation in many different career fields, including business and government. Some colleges offer a specific "liberal arts" degree for this purpose.

Fast-track options include getting credit for taking College Level Examination Programs tests (CLEP) and other college-level examinations. For more information on CLEP, access CollegeBoard.com, click on "College Board Tests" and "CLEP." Many colleges accept credit for CLEP general and subject area examinations; check with specific colleges on their CLEP policies.

Many colleges also offer "Credit for Life Experience." Adult students may obtain credit for life experience by creating a portfolio of their professional and personal experiences and accomplishments. Examples of relevant life experiences that you may be able to receive credit for include:

- running a household and raising children
- corporate training or other business skills
- professional licenses and certifications
- community involvement
- competency earned by developing or creating a product; for example, publishing articles or creating a type of software.

For more information, contact the colleges that are of interest to you.

Should You Get Your Graduate Degree?

For many stay-at-home career moms, now may be the optimal time to get your advanced degree. If you're interested in returning to college to get your master's degree, carefully consider the pros and cons of getting a graduate degree in terms of your professional career goals and the financial cost.

For example, if you have an undergraduate degree and left your career knowing that you will need more education for another promotion, then now may be the time. Or, if you are looking to make a career change, then you may want to consider getting an advanced degree. A teacher may want to get an MA to get a salary boost. A doctorate may be necessary if you're planning for a career in academia and your career goal is to become a full-time tenured professor.

Whatever your reasons, be sure to research your career objectives and talk to people in that industry about the advantages and need for a graduate degree in that career field. Important considerations include:

- Is a graduate degree necessary for entry into a certain occupation?
- If it isn't necessary, will a graduate degree improve your chances of getting that job?
- Will you be overqualified with a graduate degree?
- Will you be eligible for better promotion opportunities with a graduate degree?
- Will you receive a boost in pay? How much?
- Exactly what type of graduate degree will you need?
- Does the caliber of the school matter?

Is It Worth the Investment?

While the investment in an associate's or undergraduate degree generally pays off financially, what about a graduate degree? To find out, you should do a cost-benefit analysis by looking at the marketability of having a master's degree in the particular career field that you hope to enter. In some fields, a graduate degree is necessary or preferred. In others, an MA or MBA is "optional." In still others, the degree is largely irrelevant.

On the other hand, you may want to get a graduate degree for personal reasons—love of learning, opportunity to get out of the house, etc. If so, three cheers, just keep the financial considerations in mind when making your decision.

According to MSN financial columnist Liz Pulliam Weston, "With any degree, you should research the jobs you're likely to get with it and what they pay the first years out of school. If you're thinking of borrowing money to pay for the degree, make sure that you borrow no more, in total, than you expect to earn your first year out of school," commented Weston. "If you can't get the education you want for that price, look at alternatives: state schools instead of private, for example."

Finding the Right Degree Program

You can start your search for a graduate-degree program by accessing sites such as Peterson's: Petersons.com, click on "Graduate Schools" and the *U.S. News & World Report*, America's Best Graduate Schools: Grad-Schools.USNews.Rankings AndReviews.com/grad

When assessing grad schools, please be sure to research the reputation of a program by talking to successful professionals in that field and staff at relevant professional associations.

Should You Get Your MBA?

If you are specifically considering getting an MBA, think about getting it now. True, your future company may pay for your MBA when you go back into the workforce, but will you have the time? Fast-forward . . . your children are older—you are taking them to soccer, scouts, and so on—on top of working full time. Do you want to take classes and study on top of all that? Maybe you have a stay-at-home spouse, grandma, or nanny to help out and this will not be an issue for you. Carefully consider if you will have time to do it all and still have time for your children and spouse. If not, consider getting your MBA now—despite the cost—or forgoing getting your MBA altogether, at least for now. Perhaps you can get your MBA while working part-time later on, although you will not be able to obtain tuition assistance from your company.

ADVANTAGES OF GETTING AN MBA

If you're interested in a management career, then you may want to consider the advantages of getting an MBA. An MBA will give you the knowledge and credentials necessary to compete for high-level management jobs and/or change careers into other business industries. An MBA can give you the ticket to re-enter the corporate world after being home for a number of years. And an MBA will fill in your resume gap.

An MBA graduate will likely be given a higher salary than an applicant with only an undergraduate degree. According to some experts, the typical MBA graduate can expect to receive up to a 40 percent boost in their salary—a hefty return on their MBA investment.

According to Stacy Blackman, owner of Stacy Blackman Consulting, StacyBlackman.com, a Los Angeles-based national firm that assists clients with gaining admission to top business schools, prospective business school students should consider whether they need an MBA. "If the only motivation is to re-join the workforce, I would first check to see if a job search can be done without an MBA. MBA programs have great career services, but if you're re-entering the same industry, you might already have adequate skills, as well as a strong network and reputation you can leverage," Blackman said. "The MBA is a great tool and has many benefits but it is not the only way to re-enter the workforce and may be overkill, depending on the needs of the individual."

Prospective business school—"b-school"—candidates should consider the financial costs versus how much more money you may expect to earn with an MBA. Forbes.com has a "business school calculator" (to access the page, enter "business school calculator" into the search from the home page) where you can determine your expected five-year gain by attending b-school. On the site, you plug in the b-school that you plan to attend to get a report on how much money you may expect to earn, on average, and how much the degree will cost you.

CHOOSING AN MBA PROGRAM

Going to b-school is a big investment, and in this realm—prestige matters—depending on your career goals and objectives. If you're considering going to b-school, keep in mind that "high quality" programs may enable you to compete more effectively for better, higher-paying jobs.

To research how important it may be for you to attend a "high quality" program, you will need to do some research on your industry or intended career field. You can start by contacting relevant professionals in your personal and online networks and professionals in the industry of interest to you. Ask them about the advisability of obtaining an MBA in that career field and whether you need to attend a top school to get the type of job you're seeking. Talk to as many people as possible to get a broad range of opinions.

To find out b-school rankings, check out the MBA rankings on sites such as BusinessWeek.com, CollegeJournal.com, Forbes.com, PrincetonReview.com, and USNews.com.

Keep in mind that the practice of ranking schools is both controversial and subjective, but it's a good place to start. You'll not be surprised to see the names of the top listings: Harvard, Stanford, the University of Pennsylvania (Wharton), etc. The order will differ somewhat on all of the sites, but the same top schools appear consistently on every list.

As a stay-at-home career mom, you're probably not going to pick up and move your family somewhere else. What if you don't live near one of the "best" colleges or are not willing to relocate? Or, you don't have the academic or professional background to get into one of these programs? Your options include applying to the best b-schools in your commuting area for which you may be qualified and which you can afford, and considering MBA distance-learning programs. Several of the aforementioned sites allow you to search by geographic area. You can focus in on the "best" b-schools for the industry specialty that you plan to study.

Contact local b-schools to find out which companies recruit employees from that school. You may find that your local b-school will provide the credentials you need for getting a job at companies in your area that are of interest to you for possible future employment. You can also contact the human resources departments for companies that are of interest to you and ask them about the advisability of getting an MBA from a certain school in terms of the possibility of getting a job at that company.

"Frequently you have to create your own rankings based on your own personal criteria," Blackman said. "If someone is planning on staying in a certain geographical area, a lesser-known, local program may be the right fit—the network will be local and local companies will recruit. In this case, there would be no need to go to a big, brand name school, where your local companies may not even be recruiting."

FINDING A "MOM-FRIENDLY" MBA PROGRAM

While nearly six out of ten undergraduate students are women, the percentage of women in MBA programs hovers around 30 percent, according to a 2006 report from the Forté Foundation, a consortium of business schools and corporations working to increase the numbers of women who pursue MBAs.

MBA program recruiters have difficulty recruiting women for a number of reasons. Some women choose to forgo b-school because of sheer timing, according to industry experts. Many MBA programs require that their applicants have a number of years of industry experience before applying to their programs. The pre-requisite years of experience may coincide with the timing that a woman plans to get married and start a family. MBA programs can be very challenging and not "family friendly" in terms of the time commitment required.

According to Blackman, business schools are "definitely trying to recruit more women and lower the barriers to unrepresented groups in general. Making the MBA more accessible to mothers is one way to increase females," Blackwell said. "The biggest thing I have seen is that some schools are trying to create schedules that women with children can take advantage of, taking all classes while children are in daycare or in school."

Across the country, many b-schools have established work-life policies and programs, support groups for women and mothers, women-only executive conferences and mentoring programs, and other resources. Some b-schools have initiated a policy of admitting students right out of college or only with a year or two of work experience.

Women's Business Resources

If you're interested in getting an MBA, check out the following sites:

- Forté Foundation: ForteFoundation.org, a consortium of major corporations and top business schools. Its mission is to provide information and motivate women for business careers and educate women on the value of an MBA.
- National Association of Women MBAs: NAWMBA. org, dedicated to empowering women MBAs.

In a Mom's Own Words

*Cheryl Stein: A Canadian Mom Who Commuted Internationally
to Go to Grad School*

Cheryl Stein, a Hampstead, Quebec, mom went to grad school
to study organizational development and is now the owner
of her own career-consulting business. While in graduate
school, Stein had an "extreme commute" from her home in
Canada to Fielding Graduate University in Santa Barbara,
California. She completed most of her coursework from home
on an online basis and commuted to the California campus
once every four months.

"I was in a rotten marriage and working on and off in a family
business and knew that I had to get out. I had four young
children. I had an undergrad degree in English Literature. I
went back to get some undergrad credits in Human Relations,
which I did two years part-time, and then went to grad school
to do a masters in Organizational Development and also got
a masters certificate in coaching. I am practicing as a family
business consultant and executive coach—after four really
hard years where the kids had to get their own juice because
Mommy is writing a paper . . ."

Now an executive coach, family business consultant, and
Monster.com/Canada career columnist, Stein said that she
once thought that she was stuck in her marriage. "You're not
stuck!" she advises other moms in similar situations. For Stein,
the answer to changing her situation was to go to graduate
school in order to obtain the education and credentials needed
to establish her own successful business.

Re-married now, Stein works out of her home, enabling her to
have a flexible schedule that accommodates raising her four
children. Her educational journey may not yet be over—Stein
is now considering whether to go back to college again to get
her doctoral degree.

In a Mom's Own Words

Diane Anderson: A California Mom Who Went Back to School
for Three Degrees

Diane Anderson, a single California mom of two children, went back to college to obtain a bachelor's degree, an MBA, and a law degree. She is now a lawyer with two children in college. Her story reads like a Hollywood movie—complete with a happy ending.

"I left college just after I turned twenty, got married, and had two daughters. Everything was awesome for seven years. At twenty-nine, I thought I had everything—beautiful children, beautiful home, great business—I thought I had found success. Then, just one year later on my thirtieth birthday, through no fault of my own, I lost everything except my children. My marriage ended, our business folded, and my home was found to be located on a future EPA Environmental Superfund Site. I was also diagnosed with multiple sclerosis.

"To make ends meet, I became a courtesy clerk at the Safeway grocery store for $6 an hour. One rainy day, while pushing grocery carts into the store, an elderly man who I had never met shook his finger at me and said: 'If you don't go back to school, you'll be doing this for the rest of your life.' I began to cry. That's when I realized I had to go back to college and finish what I had started twelve years previously.

"I went back to school from 1996–2006, obtained three degrees, and best of all was able to be present in my daughter's lives. I first started going back to school to finish my BA part-time at nights while I worked at Safeway. There were days that I would wake up thinking I couldn't do it anymore. Then I would remember that it wasn't just for me, but I had a fundamentally more important reason to get out of bed—my daughters. I wanted to be my children's role model.

"Then in 2001 my Dad offered to financially help me so I went to school full time for my MBA and the law degree. Since I was fortunate that I did not need to work anymore, I was able to spend more time with my daughters while at the same time obtaining my degrees. We studied and did our homework alongside each other at the kitchen table.

"I passed the Bar exam last year and then opened my own law office. Going back to school after so much time was difficult, but during those early years it helped when I would sing in my head a mantra of the first two lines of a Helen Reddy song—'I am woman hear me roar, in numbers too big to ignore.'

"In my life I realized that someone can take everything away from you but no one can take away the knowledge you have acquired from school. I started back to college when my girls were seven and eight years old. Now my daughters are college students, my eighteen-year-old is a freshman at Claremont McKenna College, and my nineteen-year-old is a sophomore at Harvard University. The reason I got out of bed on those mornings paid off."

Thinking about Going to Law School?

If you have always dreamed of going to law school, then now may be an optimal time. But law school, whether as a full- or part-time student, will be a huge commitment in terms of time and money, so it's important to carefully consider if you really want or need a law degree.

For a comprehensive picture of the legal profession, consult the website for the American Bar Association (ABA): ABAnet. org and click on "Legal Education."

Finding Your Best Law School

As a stay-at-home career mom, you will likely consider law schools in your commuting area. It's important to access possible law schools and try to get into the "best" law school that you can. For current law school rankings, consult sources such as the rankings in the *U.S. News & World Report*, USnews.com (from the homepage, click on "Rankings" and "Best Graduate Schools" and then "Law"). You can search by ranking as well as by law specialties.

Keep in mind that rankings are subjective by nature and that you should carefully consider every possibility in your commuting area, unless you are interested in moving your family to another region to attend a particular law school. It's generally advisable to attend a law school in the state where you plan to practice law—unless you can get in and are willing to move to a "top ten" school.

ACCREDITATION STANDARDS
Be sure to check the accreditation of any law school that you are considering. In almost all states, you will be required to attend a law school that is accredited by the American Bar Association (ABA) in order to take the bar examination following graduation. For more information, consult the ABA website: ABAnet.org.

Keep in mind that, as of this writing, there were no ABA-approved law schools that provide a JD entirely through correspondence or distance learning.

Should You Do It?

Your years at home may be the perfect time to return to college to obtain a degree or take a series of courses to update your professional qualifications. By returning to college, you will enhance your resume and have the opportunity to network and make contacts with fellow students and instructors. You will keep your mind active, boost your self-confidence, and keep up-to-date with an industry. By going back to school, you can change career fields, if that is your goal.

Should you return to college? It depends upon your motivation, available time, support at home, and financial resources. It is generally advisable to ease your way in, taking one or two courses initially to see how you're able to balance studying and the demands of motherhood. Your years at home will pass anyway, so why not consider taking a few courses, completing a certificate program, or even a degree to add luster to your resume and boost your professional qualifications?

A Dose of Inspiration

Are you interested in going back to college to make a career change? Many moms have done just that. Here's what a few mom/students said about their educational journeys:

Tina Bennett—a Dallas, Texas, mom—went back to college to get her medical degree. "I'm a doctor now! My children are now ten and eighteen. When my daughter started mom's day out, I started school again. Prior to being a wife and mother, I was an executive assistant/legal assistant. I always knew I wanted to be a doctor so I took one class at a time until she was in school full time, and then I just went for it and completed close to seven years of school in four years. I am now faculty with the Carrick Institute of Grad Studies, training MD Neurologists and Audiologists for Vestibular Technologies, and I'm in private practice. And honestly, I managed a divorce my first year of grad school and finished on track regardless."

Jill Houk—a Chicago, Illinois, mom—made a career change from working in IT to being a personal chef. Houk was in the midst of a divorce when her mother asked her: "What do you *really* want to do with your life?" Without hesitation, she immediately replied, "A chef!"—to which her mom said, "Then do it!" Being a chef was her "life long passion," even though she had been in a successful IT career. Houk decided to follow her dreams and go back to college.

"When my son was four, I ended a long-term career in Information Technology sales and began culinary school. My program was full time, and it was difficult to balance school with family, but completely worth it. Not only did I graduate top of my class, I was able to open my own successful catering/personal chef business. Now I have the flexibility I need to attend to my son, and I'm in a field that I'm passionate about."

Kelly Stettner—a Springfield, Vermont, mom—went back to college to make a career change focused on the environment. "I've been a secretary for thirteen years and began a volunteer river cleanup group back in 2000 in my 'spare' time. A couple of years ago, my husband began encouraging me to get college credit for all the stuff I was learning about the river, so I looked into it. Our daughter was seven at the time, and I was pregnant with our second child during the financial aid interviews.

I will graduate with a Bachelors Degree in Liberal Arts, with a strong focus on environmental sciences and watershed science/river ecology. I still work full time, I read my books and write my papers in the evenings or during work breaks and on weekends. It's a lot of work, stresses me out regularly, but it is worth it!"

Teresa Todd—a Santa Clarita, California, mom—obtained her MBA and MA while raising her children. She used her education to launch a successful public relations firm. "My first child was born in 1983, and I was working for A.C. Nielsen. In 1986 I went back to school full time for an MBA at the University of Southern California. I graduated from USC in 1987 pregnant with my second child and started my own management consulting practice, which gave me the flexibility I needed to work from home. During the time I had my third child, I was elected to serve on the local school board and was involved in just about every volunteer organization in my regional area. In 2003 I decided to go back to school for a second Masters. This time I earned an MA in Strategic Public Relations from USC, graduating in 2005. I have started a public relations agency that is flourishing."

PART II

WORK OPTIONS TO CONSIDER

3 PART-TIME: THE IDEAL SOLUTION?

"If you bungle raising your children, I don't think whatever else you do matters very much."
—JACQUELINE KENNEDY ONASSIS, FORMER FIRST LADY OF THE UNITED STATES (1929–1994)

Are you tired of schlepping to work and feeling like "full time" as a concept has grown from forty hours a week to fifty or sixty or more? You are not alone. Over the past decade, full-time work outside the home has lost its appeal to many women, according to a 2007 research study conducted by the Pew Research Center, a nonpartisan think tank in Washington, DC. The results of the study mirror a significant national trend toward a preference for part-time work.

According to the study, six-in-ten working mothers with children younger than seventeen would prefer to work part-time, and one-in-five would prefer not working at all outside the home. Among full-time working women, only one-in-five say full-time work is ideal, which is down from 32 percent back in 1997. The mothers in the Pew survey who were most satisfied with their career situation had part-time jobs.

Nearly one-third of women with children under three years old, and more than one-quarter of women with children under eighteen work part-time, according to the U.S. Bureau of Labor Statistics. Seventy-two percent of all part-time workers are women, according to the Business and Professional Women's Foundation.

Part-Time Defined

Generally speaking, part-time workers are those who spend less than thirty-five hours on the job. Some part-time workers have a "job share" setup. If you have a job share, then you literally share your job with another part-time employee, typically splitting the time commitment and salary/benefits in half.

Flexible work scheduling or "flex time" is different—in this type of arrangement you still work forty hours. Flexible full-time arrangements include working fewer hours over more days (six or seven) or working different hours or shifts over the course of the week.

Despite outdated stereotypes of part-time jobs falling in the realm of Mc-restaurants, professional part-time jobs are becoming increasingly available in many industries. That said, some stay-at-home career moms take part-time and seasonal jobs in retail and other service industries to make some money and "get out of the house." There is nothing wrong with that, of course, keeping in mind that these types of positions are rarely resume builders and offer little or no career advancement possibilities, unless you are considering a career in retail management. Many of these types of part-time jobs have low salaries (paid hourly), and they often don't include benefits. But, hey, think about the discounts you can get at your favorite shops. I'm thinking Pottery Barn discounts . . . hmmm.

Part-Time Options Booming

Professional part-time jobs are available across many industries. In some industries, part-time positions are referred to as positions with "reduced hours." Other companies refer to their part-time employees as working "half-time" or "three-quarters time." Nearly half of all organizations let some employees move from full-time to part-time or visa-versa while remaining in their present position, according to the Families and Work Institute, a New York-based nonprofit research organization.

Professional part-time work allows women to continue on their career trajectory even if they are stepping out of the full-time workforce in order to raise their children. Allison O'Kelly, CEO and founder of Mom Corps, a national staffing firm, says that a woman can "absolutely" achieve her goals as a professional by working part-time. While it's unlikely that she will become a CEO on part-time basis, it is possible to have a successful professional career, O'Kelly said.

Part-time career prospects are particularly promising for physicians, nurses and other medical personnel, lawyers, and accountants. Other occupations that are seeing a growth in part-time positions include jobs in the corporate sector. Part-time jobs are also generally available in the service industries.

The availability of part-time jobs relates closely to the type of job and specific responsibilities. It works best with occupations that are relatively autonomous, for example, a doctor or computer programmer, and less well with occupations that require a lot of interaction with the remainder of the staff.

High Demand in Health Services
One of the shining stars in terms of growth of part-time jobs is the medical industry. This is not surprising. According to the U.S. Bureau of Labor Statistics (BLS), from 2000–2010, nine of the twenty fastest-growing occupations across the nation are concentrated in health services. These positions include:

- personal and home care aides (67 percent growth)
- medical assistants (60 percent growth)
- physician assistants (57 percent growth)
- medical records and health information technicians (54 percent growth).

Part-time workers account for more than one-third of workers in dental offices and clinics and close to 20 percent in physician's offices. Nursing is amenable to working a part-time schedule. Almost one-quarter of RNs work part-time, according to the BLS.

Part-Time: The Preferred Option Overseas

Globally, part-time seems to be the preferred work option. In the United Kingdom, 44 percent of the thirteen million women who work hold part-time jobs. According to a recent British study, women who work part-time have "greater life satisfaction" than stay-at-home mothers or full-time workers. British men, by contrast, are happier working full time.

Part-time employment is a common work setup for women in many European countries, according to the European Foundation for the Improving of Living and Working Conditions. One-third of women across the European Union worked part-time in 2002. The percentage of women working part-time varies widely in Europe, from 8.1 percent in Greece to almost 73 percent in the Netherlands.

Japan leads the way in Asia for part-time work for women, with more than 40 percent of women working part-time, according to United Nations' statistics. Other countries across the world with high percentages of women who work part-time include Australia, with just over 39 percent, and New Zealand with almost 36 percent. In Canada, nearly 28 percent of women worked part-time in 2002. These statistics are not tabulated to reflect if the jobs are professional or non-professional or if the woman would prefer a full-time position.

Many doctors work part-time because of the relatively independent nature of the job. Part-time physicians often work in practices with busy in-patient services because they can help lessen the other doctor's work loads. Physicians are not stigmatized for working part-time because of the high in-and-out mobility of the profession.

While most groups don't offer partnership to part-time employees, doctors can negotiate that possibility by having their part-time hours count toward partnership after being reinstated to full-time status, according to the American College of Physicians.

Dr. Jennifer Shu, a mother of a six-year-old boy, practices pediatrics at Children's Medical Group, P.C., in Atlanta, Georgia. She is a busy mom. She also finds time to write books focusing on children's health and parenting. Jennifer says she enjoys music, movies, skiing, Sudoku, and eating out. How does she find the time? Jennifer works part-time: she presently works two mornings a week, averaging eight hours a week.

Dr. Shu is not alone. According to the American Medical Association, one-third of female pediatricians work part-time, compared with 4 percent of male pediatricians. Most of the women who work part-time want to spend more time with young children.

In an American College of Physicians survey of family physicians, 12 percent opted to work on a part-time basis. Half of those doctors said they preferred part-time work for "family reasons."

More Flexibility for Lawyers

If you are a lawyer or in the legal profession, prospects are excellent for obtaining a temporary part-time position. Nearly all law offices allow for part-time schedules for lawyers, according to a National Association of Law Placement (NALP) report.

Networking Site for Women MDs

Physicians should check out Mom MD—Connecting Women in Medicine: MomMD.com. The site features job boards for part-time and flexible work opportunities.

In a Mom's Own Words
Jennifer Shu: A Part-time Doctor and Author

"I have a six-year-old son who is in first grade. When he was born, I took two years off. Then I went back to the practice where I had worked full time and became a 'per diem' physician, working only when any of our offices were short-staffed. I also had the option of taking evening and weekend shifts. The beauty of that setup is that I could work when I wanted and say no if I didn't want to work. No need to worry about scheduling vacations around other doctors' vacations. I didn't have insurance or other benefits, but I didn't need them since I got them from my husband. I would say I worked anywhere from zero to four days a week, with a day being about 9 or 10 a.m. to 3 or 4 p.m.

After doing that for about two years, we moved out of state. That hospital didn't have as flexible a schedule, but I was able to work about twenty-two hours per week. Two years later, we moved out of state again. I took six months off and am now averaging four to eight hours per week.

I highly recommend working part-time for several reasons if people are able to manage the financial change. On a personal level, it helps me prevent burnout by allowing me time to do things during the day (grocery shopping, laundry, post office, exercise) so I can spend quality time with my family when they are home. Professionally, I have been able to expand my medical work to writing books, appearing on television/ radio/print/web to communicate health issues to the public, and being more active with my professional organizations (as well as participating in my son's school activities and parent council).

In order for me to work part-time, our family made some financial decisions that we wouldn't have made if I were earning a full-time salary (for example, we only have one car now and live close enough that my husband can walk to work, and I can walk my son to school). To me, it's well worth the trade-offs, but that's a decision people will need to make on an individual basis."

However, according to the NALP, only 5 percent of lawyers are actually taking advantage of this opportunity. According to the survey, 4.7 percent of associates and 2.8 percent of partners were working part-time in 2006. Most lawyers working part-time were female: women represented 72 percent of the partners and 89 percent of the associates working on a part-time basis.

While some female lawyers forgo the part-time option because of fears of falling off the partnership track, industry experts say that part-time lawyers are now getting promoted and moving up the career ladder. Generally speaking, law firms would prefer their employee to work part-time on a short-term basis than lose the attorney completely.

Many firms are allowing lawyers to count their billable hours toward partnership, regardless if they were performed on a full-time or part-time basis. While it will take longer to obtain partnership, part-time lawyers are still on that road and many part-timers have become partners in law firms.

Laura Izon Powell, a Sacramento, California-based lawyer, has worked on a reduced schedule at her firm since 2003. "Working a reduced-hour schedule seemed like the best path to enable me to balance my family and my professional responsibilities. At the time, there were not many attorneys working part-time at my firm—and none of them were working moms. I first requested to work 80 percent of my billable hours for six months. Then, I asked for another six months. Then, I asked for a year. I have been 80 percent since I returned to work in October 2003. I was promoted from associate to principal attorney in January 2005. I was promoted again to shareholder (partner) in January 2007," Powell explained. "My decision has absolutely not affected my long-term career goals, but I think I am unusually blessed in this respect," she added.

Some firms are appointing in-house monitors to ensure that part-time lawyers are not overworked. There is one important caveat to consider, however—working part-time in a law firm often means forty hours, not fifty to sixty hours or more. Since nearly half, or 49 percent of law school grads are women, the trend toward allowing lawyers to work part-time will likely continue, according to industry experts.

Elizabeth Dalton Tyrrell, an Oklahoma City-based attorney, has worked on a part-time/reduced hours schedule since the birth of her third child in 1998. She said she's not sure how much longer she'll work part-time. While working part-time has had its benefits, Tyrrell said, there were also many caveats.

"The legal services industry is dynamic, and the process for advancement is continually evolving," Tyrell said. "Lawyers are competitive people in general, and working part-time means making some sacrifices, career wise. For some, it's a tough adjustment emotionally."

For More Information

If you're a lawyer, check out the website for Flex-Time Lawyers LLC: FlextimeLawyers.com.

Legal Support Personnel

Part-time opportunities for administrators, legal assistants and paralegals are available at some firms and agencies. The government projects that employment in this field will grow by 22 percent by 2016, which is much higher than the average for all occupations. Legal employers may, therefore, be increasingly open to offering flexible employment options to administrators, legal assistants, and paralegals.

Jane Braumann, a Northern Virginia mother of two, manages eight employees in a docketing department of a large intellectual property law firm with about 200 attorneys. She has been working at the firm for twenty-three years and has worked part-time for the past eleven years.

"I was hired as a full-time employee, however, since the birth of our second child in 1996, my husband and I decided that part-time employment would be better suited for us," Braumann explained. "The main reason for switching to part-time is to better balance work-life and home-life. I've had more

In a Mom's Own Words

Elizabeth Dalton Tyrrell: Part-time Lawyer, Full-time Mom

"I graduated from law school at Southern Methodist University in 1985 and began working at McAfee & Taft in Oklahoma City, where I have been ever since. . . . After the birth of my third child in 1998, I asked the firm to let me work on a part-time basis. At the time, I was already a shareholder at the firm, which made it much easier for me than had I been an associate. I have had a reduced schedule ever since.

Working on a reduced schedule has definitely affected my career because I have had less time to devote to building my practice. Also, I am making less money in my peak earning years so I either have to work longer or retire with less. However, I have been able to stay in private practice, so I am grateful. Also, I have been given some leadership opportunities with the firm so I do not feel like a second-class citizen.

I do recommend working part-time, but there are some caveats. First, it helps if everyone (at the firm and the part-time lawyer) remains flexible. My arrangement changed several times before we hit on a setup that seems to work for us. Second, it is a good idea to memorialize the agreement among the parties, even if it's just an e-mail confirming the discussion highlights. People tend to have selective memories. Also, it's best to address the hard questions head-on, especially those related to shareholder/partnership track. Have the conversation every year to make sure that everyone is on the same page.

I have the flexibility to break away and go and see my children in school plays, and I occasionally pick them up at carpool. I have been enormously lucky to have all the grandparents in town and friends to help out, too. Without that, there would be even more pressure to work on a full-time basis. Mostly, I feel some relief from the pressure to try to please everyone at the same time, which is worth a lot."

time to spend with the kids and to be more involved in their school and after-school activities. I've been fortunate in that my decision to work part-time has not affected my career in a negative way."

Part-Time Accounting Positions Growing

Part-time accounting positions are on the rise, especially because of the relatively independent nature of the work. These jobs are generally seasonal (tax season) and can be a good fit for a stay-at-home career mom. Since women comprise 55 percent of college accounting graduates with a bachelor's degree and 54 percent of graduates with a master's degree, according to the American Institute of Certified Public Accountants, the accounting industry is likely to continue to offer flexible work arrangements for women.

Brenda Leslie, an accountant in Woodstock, Georgia, works part-time as a manager in the resource management department at KPMG. She works about twenty-five hours a week, some from home and some from the office. Leslie has a great setup: she has the flexibility to determine the days and time that she works and sets up her own meetings. Leslie found her job via MomCorps.com, a company that specializes in placing moms in flexible jobs.

"One of the things that makes my job suitable for part-time is that it's somewhat seasonal, it can be done in less than forty hours a week, and with the technology available, much of it can be done remotely," Leslie said.

Beckye S. Young, a Norcross, Georgia-based accountant works for a small CPA firm providing auditing services. As a mother of four, she needs flexibility. Young works 8:30-2:00 when school is in session. When school is out, she telecommutes from home. Her company is very flexible and allows her to work from home if one of her children is sick.

"I have not yet achieved the ideal work-life balance, but am working toward that goal. The hours I work still exceed what I would like, as I bring home more work than I had anticipated. Some of this is due to the nature of an audit—tight deadlines,"

Young said. "In addition, I know some of the additional hours are due to my 'catching up' on some of the changes in the accounting field. However, as I get more experience, I anticipate moving more toward a balanced life-style."

An MBA Doesn't Have to Mean Sixty-Hour Weeks

In past decades, corporate jobs required a full-time plus commitment. Graduates of MBA programs often expected to work fifty to sixty or more hours a week and take only a short break after the birth of a child, maybe a few weeks, so as not to derail their career. Not anymore. The corporate world is becoming more flexible to the concerns of female grads.

Current trends in the corporate world are showing that MBA graduates are working on both a full-time and part-time basis at different times in their careers, while still keeping their career on track. According to recent studies, more than one-quarter of MBA grads work part-time, or plan to work part-time, at some point during their professional careers.

Teresa Evans-Hunter, a Raleigh, North Carolina, mom, has an MBA and an MS from the University of Maryland, University College. Evans-Hunter was working full time in a corporate position when she had twin girls. She quit two months after returning from maternity leave. "I was having difficulty balancing the demands of my family—in addition to the twins, we have a five-year-old son." After leaving that job, she decided to search for a professional part-time job. She is now the Membership Director for Sustainable North Carolina/NC Sustainable Business Council, a part-time professional position that she found via Balancing Professionals, a Raleigh, N.C.-based staffing firm.

Big Corporations Offer Part-Time Opportunities

Many of the nation's large corporations, including Accenture, Booz Allen Hamilton, Dow Corning, and many others offer part-time opportunities as a way to promote a better work-life balance and retain employees.

Victoria Dipalo, a Booz Allen Hamilton (BAH) associate in Northern Virginia, began working at BAH in 2002. A year later, she had her first child and began working for the company on a part-time basis.

"I completely recommend working part-time to other moms. Being able to have the balance of going into an office and being around peers and being able to take your infant to a play date is very rewarding," Diaplo said. "You are able to keep one foot in the working world and one at home. If you have the opportunity and work out the details, being a part of your child's life at an early age is just wonderful."

Part-Time Opportunities in IT

If you are in IT, then you may be in luck. Computer-industry jobs are often well adaptable for part-time work. This is particularly true of IT jobs that do not require a lot of personal interaction with others in your company or face-to-face meetings with clients. Part-time telecommuting opportunities are often able to be set up because of the independent nature of this profession.

Academia—A Bastion for Part-Time Work

Working as an adjunct instructor is an excellent way for stay-at-home career moms to maintain their exposure and gain teaching experience. According to the National Center for Education Statistics, almost half of the faculty at colleges and universities nationwide are in part-time positions.

Benefits for Part-Time Employees?

Some companies, including Dupont, General Mills, Merck, and others offer benefits to professional employees who reduce their work hours to part-time. To find out more, check out Working Mother's 100 Best Companies: WorkingMother.com, click on "Best Companies."

Part-Time Librarian Link

Current or future part-time librarians should check out the Association for Part-Time Librarians: Part-Time-Librarians.net

But, the caveat is that there is little job stability from semester to semester, according to the American Association of University Professors, and adjuncts typically don't receive paid benefits. That said, it can be an excellent way to start or maintain your career at a college or university.

Full-time faculty positions at universities are generally very flexible in terms of time commitment and work hours. After obtaining tenure, many college professors are able to create flexible schedules that allow for teaching, writing, research, advising students, and travel. While a doctoral degree is generally required at many four-year universities and colleges, most community colleges hire instructors with a master's degree in the subject area in which they'll be teaching.

Administration positions at universities and colleges may also be available part-time or as a job share. For example, two moms, Anna Millar and Meghan Gosk, have shared the position of associate director of the University of North Carolina's Kenan-Flagler Business School MBA Program for the past four years. Each associate director works twenty hours per week.

"We have been so happy with our job-share arrangement in that it enables us to nuture our careers while simultaneously allowing us to spend time with our families," said Gosk. "We feel strongly that these types of flexible work arrangements can and do work in the business arena and should be available to more employees."

Anna Millar has four children ranging from three years old to eleven years old. She has an MBA from Harvard Business School. Meghan Gosk has two daughters, ages seven and nine.

She has a doctorate from North Carolina State University in higher education administration. Both women worked full time after having children, but determined that the schedule did not afford them sufficient time for their families.

How did they get the position? They asked for it. The women put together a job-share proposal for their supervisor and the rest of the administration at the Kenan-Flagler Business School. Their proposal outlined the benefits of the position for the school as well as how the position would be structured. Both had worked at the school and were "known entities."

"Our mantra is prove your value, know what you want, and don't be afraid to ask for it," Millar said.

Restaurant/Retail/Hospitality Industries

Service industries, including restaurant, retail, and hospitality have been the traditional bastion for part-time careers. There are an array of sales, management, and other nonprofessional and professional positions that fall under the umbrella of service industries. Management-training programs are often available for motivated employees.

If you're looking for a part-time job in order to cover your family's health insurance, keep in mind that a growing number of retail enterprises are reportedly offering benefits to their part-time employees, including Nordstrom, Barnes and Noble, IKEA, Starbucks, and others. Part-time benefits vary, but may include healthcare plans, vacation time, retirement plans, and merchandise discounts. In many of these companies, employees are required to work a minimum number of hours per week and have completed a certain number of total hours for the benefits package to kick in.

Nonprofits

Nonprofit organizations may be amenable to part-time and other flexible work setups and could help you launch a rewarding career. You may be able to obtain a position via volunteering at that organization. Check out the following websites for nonprofit jobs:

- Chronicle of Philanthropy: Philanthropy.com/jobs
- Idealist: Idealist.org
- Nonprofit Career Network: NonprofitCareer.com

Uncle Sam's Treasure Trove of Part-Time Possibilities

The U.S. government offers part-time professional jobs across occupational fields and agencies throughout the country. Job seekers can check out part-time opportunities through USA jobs.gov.

The federal government also encourages work-life balance for current government employees. Government employees should visit the website for the Office of Personnel Management (OPM) Office of Work-Life Programs: OPM.gov/employment_and_benefits/worklife/index.asp and the link on this page to the Federal "Part-Time Employment and Job Sharing Guide." The guide includes advice on how to turn a full-time job into a part-time position and how to set up a job share.

According to the OPM, the typical part-time federal employee is almost forty-three years old and has worked for the government for ten years. Nearly 42 percent have a BA or higher, and slightly more than 72 percent are women. But less than 2 percent of part-time employees are supervisors or managers.

Part-time work is encouraged in the federal government to "balance routine and/or unexpected work and family demands." Part-time employees under permanent appointments are eligible, on a pro-rated basis, for the same benefits as full-time employees: leave, retirement, and health and life insurance coverage.

Pros and Cons of Part-Time Work

The chief advantage of part-time work is that you have more time to spend with your family. At that same time, part-time work enables a woman to continue her career and, in some cases, stay on track toward promotions and general advancement. A part-time employee keeps her feet in the working world and may find it less difficult to transition to a full-time job later on.

On the flip side, many part-time workers complain that they work full-time hours while being paid part-time wages. Technology, from cell phones to BlackBerries and the Internet, makes it possible to be "on call" 24/7. Boundaries are important. It's difficult for many part-time employees to say, "No, I am off today." Some part-time moms complain they are left out of the decision-making loop at work.

On the home front, some moms complain that their non-working time is spent doing chores and running errands. A Brandeis University study found that switching to part-time can hurt a marriage. According to the study, marital satisfaction generally declined for the part-time working women they surveyed because the women felt they had to do the housework during their time off, while their full-time working husbands failed to chip in.

But, according to a recent study published in the journal *Family Relations*, overall, part-time professionals have less work-to-family conflict and strain than full-time professionals. According to the survey, there was less job-related travel, unnecessary work, and work-to-family conflict, and greater work-family success, childcare satisfaction, and family success.

However, as in the Brandeis study, the survey found that mothers expressed disatisfaction with the more traditional division of labor in household responsibilities and less career opportunity and overall work success.

Part-time professionals receive less pay and benefits on a per-hour basis than their full-time counterparts. Benefits may be pro-rated and eliminated entirely. This may not be a significant issue for some women if their spouse has an adequate benefits package that covers health insurance and other necesssary benefits.

Part-time working moms complain about commuting times and the cost of transportation, clothing, lunches, etc., since they do not have a full-time income to pay for these incidentals.

Daycare is a big concern. It's very difficult to find a quality daycare that will admit children part-time. Some moms resort to paying for full-time care or using home care, though a nanny may be prohibitively expensive for many. Some moms take their children to home daycare centers or rely on family members to watch their children while they're working.

Summer break and school vacations pose another problem. Most part-timers are not off in the summer and must find care for their children. It's important to do a cost-benefit analysis to ensure that the high cost of care during the summer doesn't trump the wages earned during the school year.

The Hunt Is On

If you're seeking a part-time position, take a look at online job boards, including MonsterJobs.com, CareerBuilder.com, and others. Check out part-time listings on CraigsList.com, Indeed.com, and SimplyHired.com. You can designate "part-time" in the search term, and multiple opportunities should appear, depending on your industry and location.

You can find "mom friendly" companies by checking out Working Mother Magazine's annual list of the "100 Best Companies" at WorkingMother.com. On the site, you will find companies that offer part-time positions, job sharing, telecommuting, flexible work schedules, and more. Companies can be searched by category: academic institutions, financial services, hospitals and healthcare, information technology and technology services, insurance, legal services, manufacturing and retail, media, publishing and advertising, pharmaceutical and biotech, and professional services. You can enter the term "part-time" or "job share" into the search, and the matching companies will appear. On the site, you can find companies that offer benefits to part-time employees. Company websites can also be accessed via the site.

Many staffing companies assist job seekers looking for part-time positions. To find out about flexible job searching sites and more about how to find a part-time job, go to Chapter Ten: "Are You Ready? How to Transition Back to the Part-Time or Full-Time Workforce."

As with any job search, it's critically important to try to find jobs by networking with friends, family, former co-workers, and others. You can also make contacts when networking at professional associations. Most part-time jobs are never advertised and can be found most effectively via networking. For more information on networking, review Chapter One.

Abracadabra! How to Create a Part-Time Job

Okay, it's not as easy as saying "Abracadabra," but it's sometimes possible to create a part-time job at your present workplace. Here is the secret: make yourself indispensable to your company so that they will not say no.

Keep in mind that you have a better chance if you have worked at a company for at least a year. Employers tend to be more receptive to creating part-time jobs for those that have "paid their dues" by demonstrating capability in the traditional setting.

When considering a part-time job proposal, keep in mind that some bosses and colleagues object to part-time work because they worry that it will disrupt their business. There may be a concern that work may not get done on time or that other people will have to pick up the slack for part-timers when they're not there. Part of your goal is to convince your boss and colleagues that you can do your job effectively on a part-time basis without creating more work for them.

If you're considering a job share, keep in mind that your employer may be amenable to a job share because two suitably matched partners should bring two different skill sets to one position. Job-share setups can reduce the time that an employer needs to spend on recruitment, retention, and training.

Job shares tend to work best with positions that have clearly defined roles. It works less well with jobs that involve a lot of travel or that have unpredictable hours.

Job sharing is a good option for people who work well as a team. It's not a good option if an employee likes to exert control or needs to be rewarded for their individual performance.

It's important to devise a strategy or proposal for restructuring your job into a part-time position. Here are five steps for creating a part-time job proposal:

1. Keep a detailed record of your responsibilities at work, and then consider how your tasks might be done efficiently on a part-time basis.
2. Research information about your salary and benefits. Calculate if you can afford to live with reduced benefits: vacation pay, retirement, and health insurance.
3. Research policies and practices at your company about part-time work. Consult your company's human resources manual or pages on their website detailing part-time policies. If there are currently no part-time policies in place, take that into account when formulating your own proposal. Emphasize the cost-saving component for the employer.
4. Develop your strategy. Consider the possibility of proposing a job share. In some cases, you may be required to find a partner who could share your job with you.
5. Make a written proposal to your supervisor. In some less formal offices, you may want to make your pitch verbally. Remember: "timing is everything." Try to strategize the best time to make your proposal. Focus on the needs of your employer, not your own needs, and how you can get your job done efficiently on a part-time basis. Make it a win-win proposal. Suggest a "trial run" so that the employer can evaluate whether the arrangement is working.

Remember, a part-time staff offers many advantages to an employer. Companies save office space and costs by hiring multiple part-time employees who rotate their time, and many companies find that retaining quality employees is more economical than hiring and retraining new employees. In other words, allowing you to go part-time reduces "brain drain"—so make yourself indispensable to an organization if you want to work part-time.

Is part-time your ideal solution? It depends upon your perspective. For some, it's the best of both worlds. Other moms find it stressful and not financially lucrative. Some stay-at-home career moms choose to forgo the part-time experience and work completely from home, either on a telecommuting basis for a company or by establishing their own business. Others find a hybrid solution by telecommuting from home at least a part of their full-time work week. All of these options are also viable, but important considerations need to be taken to make these options work for you.

4 TELECOMMUTING—SHOULD YOU CATCH THE WAVE OF THE FUTURE?

"Life is to be lived. If you have to support yourself, you had bloody well better find some way that is going to be interesting. And you don't do that by sitting around wondering about yourself."

—KATHERINE HEPBURN, ACTRESS, (1907–2003)

Telecommuting, or working at home via computer, is becoming an increasingly popular way to work. Also termed as "telework," "virtual work," "distance work," or "remote work," telecommuting can be an ideal setup for stay-at-home career moms because they can work out of their home office. The good news is that telecommuting enables you to eliminate your commuting times, manage your schedule, and, well, wear your most comfortable clothing—think: pajamas. The caveat is that you may still need childcare.

Some teleworkers work from other locations. For the purposes of this chapter, telecommuting means that you are employed by someone else and work at home, at least some days, for that company via your home computer.

Stay-at-home career moms might want to consider working part-time on a telecommuting basis as a strategy to "keep in the game." By telecommuting, you are not leaving your company and will still have your name known among your co-workers and customers. You will maintain your links to your organization, even by working only one day per week.

But while there are an increasing number of part-time telecommuting opportunities, most employed telecommuters work full time by working one to three days per week out of their home and going into the office the remaining days. Two days per week at home and three at the office is the national average among teleworkers, according to the International Telework Association.

"Telework programs are a great tool to attract new talent and keep existing ones," said Anne Ruddy, president of WorldatWork. "Time is the new currency," Ruddy commented. "Many workers are dual focused on both work and family so that a premium is placed on flexibility over money."

Chuck Wilsker, president and CEO of the Telework Coalition, added, "People are more productive and work longer hours when they telecommute. Employers can hire people from more geographically diverse areas."

Telecommuting is a growing trend for both women and men. In a recent study conducted by the Polling Company, Inc./ WomanTrend, 62 percent of American workers surveyed who do not presently have the option to work remotely (including current workers and those planning to join the workforce within three years), said they would prefer to have the option to work remotely in their current or next job.

"Flexible scheduling and the ability to work outside the traditional office setting is increasingly valued as they try to master—or just manage—that elusive work-life balance," commented Kellyanne Conway, President and CEO of the Polling Company/Woman Trend.

An estimated 23.5 million employed Americans worked from home at least one day per month in 2003, according to the International Telework Association and Council (ITAC). WorldatWork estimates that there will be 100 million U.S. teleworkers by 2010.

The Upside to Telecommuting

There are many advantages to working as a telecommuter. Chief among them is that you can work from anywhere—at home, at Grandma's, on a plane, on a Caribbean island . . . (Okay, that might be going a little too far.) You can work during your peak energy hours, giving you more flexibility to schedule time with family and friends.

Other advantages include improved job satisfaction. Overall, employee job satisfaction is "highest among teleworkers and their managers," up to 25 percent more as compared to in-office employees, according to Ruddy.

Other advantages include:

- Less stress
- Reduced exposure to "office politics" (three cheers for that one!)
- Fewer interruptions from co-workers
- Increased physical comfort: you control the heat, a/c, lighting, etc.

You will also save money on lunch, clothing, dry cleaning, fuel, parking, tolls, public transportation, and more. Your commuting time will be reduced or eliminated.

As a stay-at-home career mom, your main interest here may be on saved childcare costs. You may or may not be able to avoid paying for daycare if you are a telecommuter. Many companies require that another person is present and responsible for your child's care if that child is a baby or preschooler. You may need to hire a nanny, au pair, etc., to help you with your child while you're working. Why? In most jobs, it's impossible to focus attention on your work if you're trying to simultaneously work and care for your child. It isn't fair to your employer or your child. You cannot maintain professional credibility if your baby has a melt down in the background while you're talking to a client.

Kathleen J. Wu, a Dallas, TX, lawyer/partner and expert on issues facing women in the workplace, said it's "absolutely" essential for telecommuters to have childcare while they're working at home. "You can't think with screaming kids in the background," Wu said. "If you've ever tried to make a phone call with your kids in the house, you know this already. They could ignore you all day, but the minute you get on the phone, they have a crisis they absolutely must talk to you about. Besides, SpongeBob just isn't a very good babysitter."

Most moms are okay with having on-site childcare because they enjoy working at home. The child's caregiver can bring the baby to them for a feeding, and the mom can take breaks to spend time with their child. The best part is being able to observe the interaction between the child and the caregiver to see if it's an optimal relationship. You may be able to hire a caregiver who also does housework, eliminating some of those chores for you and your spouse. Other moms choose to put their child or children in daycare.

If you're telecommuting part-time, you may be able to schedule your work around naps and your spouse's schedule, depending upon the particular job and your child. Some children nap at predictable times—others are like the "Energizer Bunny" and take brief naps whenever. But what happens if your normally predictable child wakes up during a conference call? For this reason, most moms seek childcare for children under five or six.

Telecommuting is a good option for moms with older children, according to Conway. "Telecommuting is not just for the new mom or the women whose children are in the pre-K tender-age range," Conway said. "We have witnessed an increase in the number of women whose pre-teen and teenage children seem to need or desire a more direct and regular maternal presence during those at-risk hours between 3 and 6 p.m. structure their days to accommodate this."

Moms with school-age children might be able to tele-commute without hiring childcare. Many stay-at-home career moms work during the hours that their children are in school. Some moms might work a later shift after their spouse returns home and takes over the supervision of the children; this often works well with telecommuters who interact with clients in other time zones.

As a telecommuter, you may be able to arrange your workload so that you can attend school activities or work at home if your child is ill. Telecommuters are often paid the same as an on-site worker, but may or may not receive benefits.

The Downside of Telecommuting

According to a Woody Allen quote, "80 percent of life is just showing up." The main disadvantage to telecommuting is that you are not there: "out of sight, out of mind." According to some studies, it may hinder your advancement opportunities in a company. That said, many telecommuters work at home several days and in the office the rest of the time, so this may be less of an issue for you.

Your co-workers may also resent what they see as "preferential treatment," according to a recent study. You'll need to find ways to interact with them and show them that you're actually working, not loafing, while at home.

These trust issues may spill over into other areas within the company's hierarchy. Some "old school" managers just don't get it. They want to be able to track your every movement and have a hands-on management philosophy. Chances are that if you work for that type of company, you won't be allowed to telecommute anyway. They probably don't have a telecommuting option and might not even consider a proposal to telecommute.

Employers have a number of concerns about initiating telecommuting work arrangements, according to recent studies. Important considerations include:

- Security: A company may be concerned about the confidentiality of privileged information. Precautions against hacking and theft would need to be in place.
- Technology: Who will be there if your computer breaks? Most companies have in-office computer technicians, who may or may not make house calls.

- Team building: How can managers work on team-building and cooperative-work arrangements with a dispersed staff?

As a telecommuter, you should make an effort to maintain communication with colleagues by e-mailing or telephoning them with relevant updates and information. Telecommuters may also be required to attend some or all company meetings.

One complaint many telecommuters have is that they sometimes get lonely and feel isolated from other adults. That's another reason it's important to stay connected to your online professional networks and to get out of the house to meet people face-to-face. A quick solution for the loneliness factor is to occasionally take your laptop to the local coffee shop or to the community library and work from there.

Telecommuters should also attend professional association meetings and go to conferences. This will enable you to have face time with other people in your career field. You could also join or start a local network or club with other home-based workers.

Stay-at-home career moms often say that they have difficulty balancing work life and home life. They can become addicted to working and be on the computer constantly. Here is where a telecommuter needs to set a schedule and stick to it. You'll need to establish boundaries with your employer and have the will power to make transitions between working and being at home.

Another problem for stay-at-home career moms: the refrigerator! It beckons from across the room or down the stairs. Ditto for housework, neighbors stopping by, watching Oprah, and so on. Again, it's mandatory to set up a rigid work schedule and stick to it. Friends and neighbors need to know you're working and can't be interrupted. Think: caller ID. Keep the television off, tape your favorite television shows, and stay away from the refrigerator. Can you do it? It depends upon your particular personality. Take the following quiz for more insight into whether you should consider working at home.

TWENTY QUESTIONS: SHOULD YOU TELECOMMUTE?

Directions: Consider the following questions. If your answer to any question is "no," then carefully evaluate if you believe you are a good candidate for a telecommuting setup.

1. Are you self-disciplined?
2. Can you prioritize your tasks?
3. Can you work independently without a lot of input from others?
4. Are you up-to-date with technology?
5. Do you get lonely when you're not around people?
6. Will you be able to set a work schedule and stick to it?
7. Are you assertive enough to stop neighbors and friends from interrupting your work?
8. Do you love your job?
9. Do you enjoy the daily responsibilities that you do in your job?
10. Are you good at writing e-mails?
11. Do you have good telephone skills?
12. Can you stop yourself if you have the urge to do housework or other nonwork activities during work hours?
13. Can you focus on your work responsibilities without goofing off?
14. If you have an at-home caregiver, will you be able to let them take care of your child or children most of the time while you're working?
15. If you have older children, can you keep them occupied while you're working during school vacations, summer break, etc.?
16. If someone else is at home, including a spouse or parent, will you be able to work effectively without interruptions from them?
17. Can you set boundaries between your work and personal life?
18. Is your boss the type of person who will trust that you're working?
19. Will you be able to complete all of your work responsibilities

without needing colleagues to take over some of your duties?

20. Are you *absolutely* positive you will not be bored when working at home?

Top Jobs for Telecommuting

Some jobs are more amenable to telecommuting than others; for example, a position with a lot of in-person customer interaction would not be conducive to this arrangement. The best jobs for telecommuting tend to be jobs that are performed on an independent basis. Here are some samples:

- Accountant, auditor, tax professional
- Artist, designer, graphic illustrator
- Call-center jobs, virtual customer service, receptionist, technical-help operator
- Coding and transcription
- Computer-related professions: programmer, web designer
- Education: online instructor or tutor
- Editorial: writer, editor, proofreader
- Financial analyst
- Lawyer/paralegal/litigation coder
- Nurse (telephone advice)
- Office work/administrative: virtual assistant or secretary
- Public relations professional
- Recruiter
- Researcher
- Sales professional

Spotlight: Working as a Virtual Assistant

Stay-at-home career moms with administrative experience might consider becoming a virtual assistant. Virtual assistants can work for one client as a telecommuter or for many clients on a freelance basis. Via the Internet, virtual assistants can work for clients anywhere on the globe.

"Virtual assistants can do most tasks that an in-house assistant can do," said Melody Spier, a mom and owner of

Essential Office Support, a Tennessee-based global agency. "Some offer research, ghost writing, customer support, transcription, website creation and maintenance, bookkeeping, human resource tasks, marketing assistance, and more. Basically, anything that can be done over the Internet, through fax, phone or even mail could be a service that a virtual assistant may want to offer."

Virtual assistants work for clients via telephone, fax, and Internet. Most virtual assistants work for individuals or small businesses that need secretarial help, and there are many opportunities in this growing field. To find out more, check out the websites for organizations such as the International Virtual Assistant Association: IVAA.org and the International Association of Virtual Office Assistants: IAVOA.com.

Spotlight: Lawyers and Telecommuting
Some legal jobs are well-suited to working on a telecommuting basis, and that industry is showing signs of allowing an increasing number of lawyers and legal assistants to do so.

Deborah Epstein Henry, founder and president of Flex-Time Lawyers, LLC, a national consulting firm focused on work-life balance and the retention and promotion of women attorneys, said that while some law firms are allowing telecommuting, it "generally hasn't fully rolled out in firms." She noted, however, that the legal industry could be well-suited to telecommuting because billable hours could be generated from anywhere. "We are hopeful and optimistic for change," she said.

"Although no single work arrangement is ideal for all people, I think telecommuting can be an outstanding setup for many lawyers," commented Nicole Belson Goluboff, an attorney, telecommuting advocate, and author of *The Law of Telecommuting* and *Telecommuting for Lawyers*.

"Lack of 'face time' need not hurt promotion potential in firms. But it can if the firm has not developed its telework program in a well-thought-out way or has not received adequate training concerning telework," Goluboff added. "When firms implement wide-scale telework programs, everyone at the firm—including both those who will telecommute and those who will not—must be trained to handle the new business strategy. One topic training must cover is how to manage by objective, rather than physical oversight."

For More Information

Information about telecommuting and the legal profession can be accessed via:

- Flex-time Lawyers, LLC, FlextimeLawyers.com
- NALP (the Association for Legal Career Professionals), NALP.org

Spotlight: Sales: Why Pay for Office Space?

Salespersons are often in the field and don't always require office space. Many high-end sales companies allow their account executives to telecommute and check in with the office for training or meetings. Telecommuting opportunities are sometimes available in a range of fields, including pharmaceutical sales, office equipment sales, mortgage sales, and others.

Corporate Telecommuting: Opportunities Are Growing

Telecommuting opportunities are available at many corporations nationwide, although most telecommuters will have started their career working on-site. An increasing number of employees start as telecommuters, however. Nadine G. Monaco, a communications professional for MITRE Corporation, a mother of two sons, was hired to work on a part-time telecommuting basis. She works twenty-four to thirty hours a week, two days on-site and one day on a telecommuting basis from home.

Monaco said she found her job through networking. She had worked for nine years in the industry at another company on a full-time basis before having her children. After the birth

In a Mom's Own Words
Nicole Belson Goluboff, Telecommuting Attorney/ Mom

"I had experience as a telecommuting litigator when my first child was under two years old. I negotiated my telework arrangement with a firm where I had not previously been employed. I committed to work part-time, although my hours quickly approached a full-time schedule. I did not have a regularly scheduled day in the office: I spent all my working hours at home, going into the office—or court—only as necessary.

"My son was a generous napper during the day and went to sleep for the night early (although he did not sleep through the night until he was almost a year old). I was generally able to work when he slept and to spend concentrated time with him when he was awake. Although I slept little and occasionally received hard-to-juggle work-related calls during the hours my son was awake, on the whole, I felt enormously pleased to be doing the kind of professional work I loved without having to give up time I considered invaluable with my son. While I did not have outside childcare in place at the time, I now consider it important for a telecommuter to have such care available during any hours she expects to work. At the same time, I would have some concerns about the legality of an employer mandating such care expressly in a telework policy or agreement.

"Before my son was born, my work hours were such that I spent virtually no time at home. I did not want to continue that schedule as a parent, and I wanted to maximize every hour of the day—either by meeting work or family goals. Working from home seemed the best solution for me, and it turned out to be.

"Since I decided to leave my position at the firm to which I telecommuted (for reasons having nothing to do with the telework arrangement), I have been self-employed and working from home. I now have two sons and continue to find that a home office enables me to meet both my work and life goals."

of her first son, she went to work on a part-time basis. After six years, that company wanted her to work full time, so she left and came to MITRE eight years ago and continued on her part-time schedule. Monaco now enjoys the flexibility of working both on-site and at the company. Monaco said it's the "best of both worlds" and that she needed very minimal childcare.

In a Mom's Own Words

Marie Risser: Telecommuting Professional/Mom

Marie Risser, an associate at Booz Allen Hamilton, started her career at her company's headquarters and transitioned to working entirely on a telecommuting basis after about fifteen months.

"I joined Booz Allen in June of 1999 straight out of college. Part of my job description was travel, and I found myself traveling a week every other month. It was during these times of travel that I learned about telecommuting and realized how much you can be 'in touch' with the office without physically being there.

"In October of 2000, I got married. My husband has a fairly unique profession, so we needed to move to the location of his work, which was about 200 miles from the office from which I was working. Devastated at the potential loss of my fascinating job, I started to talk to managers and colleagues about the possibility of working from remote. After all, I had been traveling for larger and larger portions of my time; they might not notice a whole lot of difference. Luckily, I had forward-thinking managers who were pleased with my job performance so far and were willing to take the risk.

"I set out from that point with very clear strategies and communication and have built an eight-year career off the fifteen-sixteen month [startup] period I spent in the physical office in Virginia. I've earned an additional promotion and been given organizational responsibilities for both the team at large of one hundred people and more direct, managerial responsibility for a smaller team of six to eight people; all of the folks who I manage also have unique work situations, or flexwork situations. As a telecommuter, I've worked full time, and I've worked part-time.

"Since developing a telecommuting position with the firm, I've since had three kids. One thing that most folks find fascinating about this is that none of them has ever spent a single hour in daycare. Even after our five-year-old twin girls were born, I was still able to work full time for almost a year. Telecommuting gives a great deal of flexibility to when you can work and that's been a real lifesaver. Our son was born nineteen months ago and has joined his sisters in a household where Mom occasionally has to 'take a meeting' while changing a diaper or serving a meal."

Finding a Reputable Telecommuting Job

There are two ways to find a telecommuting job. The first is to try to get your present or recent employer to allow you to work on a telecommuting basis. This is the easiest and generally the best avenue to finding a telecommuting job.

According to recent reports, some companies are becoming increasingly open to the possibility of hiring telecommuters on a full-time basis without requiring the traditional prerequisite of having to work for the company for a few years. While these types of opportunities can be difficult to find, there is a growing trend toward hiring people on a telecommuting basis.

But, there are also a myriad of scams to watch out for when looking for telecommuting jobs via the web. Here you may have to navigate virtual landmines while trying to find a reputable job. We are all bombarded with spam that reads: "work at home!" "stuff envelopes for $100 a day!" "assemble crafts for big money!" etc. The best advice to you is to completely ignore these job ads. Most, if not all of them, are scams. In most cases, they will ask you to send money to apply for the job and to pay for required training or supplies. This is not a job. A job will pay you, not the other way around. Here is the most important rule to follow for avoiding scams: *NEVER PAY TO GET A JOB.*

Finding Telecommuting Jobs on the Web

One of the best aspects of telecommuting is that you can apply for a job anywhere, unless the job requires occasional "face time" or working in the office a number of days per week. Some jobs are not "time specific," that is, you can set your own schedule. Other jobs operate on a schedule. You may want to do some creative scheduling and look for positions in different time zones when a family member is home to watch the children.

Positions with telecommuting benefits can be found via the traditional "big" job boards such as Monster.com, HotJobs. com, and CareerBuilder.com, as well as many specialized and

How to Spot a Scam

To spot a scam, start by checking the following sites:

- Better Business Bureau: BBB.org
- Work at Home Schemes, Federal Trade Commission Facts for Consumers: FTC.gov/ bcp/edu/pubs/consumer/invest/inv14.shtm
- Work at Home Scams, the National Consumer's League Internet Fraud Watch: Fraud.org/tips/internet/workathome.htm

Tip: The first step to finding a reputable job is to remember that "work at home" or "telecommuting" is not a job. A reputable job will be advertised as "accountant," "receptionist," etc.—not "work at home accountant." "Work at home" may be listed under benefits, but not as the main component of the job.

smaller niche sites. CraigsList.com is a popular site for finding telecommuting positions. Telecommuting jobs with the Federal government can be found by accessing JobSearch.USAjobs.gov and designating "telecommuting" as a keyword in the search.

Access other job-posting sites by searching "telecommuting jobs" using any search engine. Sites targeted for moms can be found by searching "moms" and "telecommuting jobs." Remember to check all sites out carefully and be vigilant for scams. You should never pay money for work-at-home employment. While there are some legitimate sites that charge viewers to access their lists of job openings, be sure that these sites don't guarantee that you'll get a job or try to "sell" jobs. Remember, there are many sites with free listings on the Internet.

Telecommuting opportunities in both Canada and the United States can be accessed via the Canadian Telework Association website: IVC.ca, click on "Jobs" and then on "Finding a Telework Job." The Telework Coalition maintains a page with links to telecommuting job listings: TELCOA.org, click on "Telework Jobs and Opportunities."

Telecommuting positions can also be found via sites such as Indeed.com and SimplyHired.com. On either of these sites, you can designate "telecommute" and "telecommuting" as keywords in your search when using the advanced search. On SimplyHired.com, you can click on "Special Searches" and then "Mom Friendly Companies," a section of the site that is produced in partnership with *Working Mother* magazine.

Working Mother magazine's website, WorkingMother.com, is useful for finding job leads. Click on "100 Best Companies" to access profiles of the top one hundred companies judged by the magazine as "family friendly." According to the site, all of the included companies now offer telecommuting on a part-time basis; this contrasts to the national figures, which indicate that only 33 percent of America's companies offer telecommuting.

Fortune magazine's annual "100 Best Companies" list includes a link to companies that allow employees to telecommute at least 20 percent of the time. In 2008, eighty-four of the one hundred companies listed allowed telecommuting. Access the site via this link: money.CNN.com/magazines/fortune/bestcompanies/best_benefits/telecommuting.html

You May Have to Start On-Site

In many cases, however, you may have to start working at a company on-site and then try to negotiate a telecommuting position. Applicants with skills that are in high demand, for example, an expert in certain types of software design or financial analysis, may have an easier time finding a direct-hire telecommuting job, according to Gil Gordon, a telecommuting expert. Working at home is generally considered a "perk." As with finding any job, you need the right skills and experience. Gordon suggests working at a company for a "minimum of six months" before trying to negotiate a telecommuting setup.

As with any job search, the best way to find a job is via networking (see Chapter One). Remember as you conduct your job search that your potential new employer is going to be focusing first on your qualifications and skills. Of secondary importance will be your need or desire to work at home. Yes, you will save them some overhead costs and possibly benefits, but their number one priority will be if you can get the job done.

Negotiating Telecommuting Options

Check and see if your company already has a telecommuting policy in place as your first course of action. If so, you are in luck, follow the procedures outlined in the employee manual and/or on the company website. Federal government workers should access the Office of Personnel's Telework site: Telework.gov. Click on "How should I ask for permission to telework?"

If there is no telecommuting policy in place, try to find out if other employees have or are working on a telecommuting basis. Talk to them about their experience telecommuting with the company and how they arranged for the setup.

If you can't find another telecommuter, then you may be a "trailblazer" for your company. In this case, you should give your management a written and verbal proposal requesting the opportunity to telecommute. Your oral presentation will give your boss the opportunity to ask questions and raise objections to you in person. The written proposal will allow them to take time to consider it and present it to other management.

Make sure you focus your request on how telecommuting can help *them*, not *you*. In other words, don't say you want to telecommute to be home with the kids, take care of your parents, etc. Instead, come up with a proposal on how your company will benefit. Be sure to focus on:

- Improved productivity and job performance. Telecommuting will enable you to distance yourself from time-wasting office distractions such as chatty co-workers.
- Real-estate savings—Employers save money on office space, parking space, and equipment. Office space for the average worker in North America costs $10,000 per year, according to the Telework Coalition.
- Less missed time—telecommuters tend to miss less work time for illness and because of weather closings. They may also be able to work despite transit strikes, flooding and natural disasters, and other emergencies.
- Compliance with any applicable state-mandated regulations/laws for providing telecommuting opportunities.
- Potential for tax credits and other incentives.
- Helping the environment by reducing traffic congestion and emissions. For statistics and information, check out: the telecommuting web page for the Clean Air Council: CleanAir.org/transportation/greenCommute.html.

Be sure to focus on how you can get your job done and how your performance can be tracked and evaluated. You may want to suggest a "trial run" so that both you and your management will have a period of time to evaluate if telecommuting is working out for both of you. It is advisable to request working one to two days at home and then suggest increasing the number of days later on if it is acceptable to both you and your employer. If you have very young children, consider explaining how your childcare needs will be covered.

Sample Telecommuting Proposal

1. Introduction

In the introduction, state your objective: telecommuting one or more days per week. Include a concise statement as to why you would like to telecommute. Be sure to focus on the benefits to the company—financial and in terms of your productivity. Site statistics and benefits detailed in this chapter and via the website links. Do not mention saved childcare costs or any other benefit to you.

Provide an overview of your key contributions to the company. Emphasize your value to the company.

2. Your Job Description

Provide an overview of your job description and your daily responsibilities. Detail which responsibilities can be done at home and which need to be done in the office. Describe any accommodations or changes in your job description that you are proposing. It's advisable to keep these proposed changes to a minimum.

3. Proposed Work Schedule

Provide a detailed proposal of which days/hours you hope to work in the office and what days/hours you would like to work at home. State your availability for meetings and other company activities. It may be advisable to suggest working one to two days at home initially as a trial run.

4. Equipment

List the equipment and resources that you already have in your home and any equipment that you will need the company to provide. Be clear about any requests for equipment, supplies, or services, including tech support.

5. Performance Evaluation

Detail how your supervisor can monitor and evaluate your performance.

6. Closing

Thank your supervisor and management for their consideration of your proposal. Again suggest a trial run so that everyone can determine if this arrangement will work.

Your Tech Setup

According to Chuck Wilsker, president and CEO of the Telework Coalition, "We believe that technology is about a third of the telework picture along with well-thought-out policies, processes, and procedures (we call it P³). That said, without evolving technologies we would not have telework and telecommuting as we know them. Many companies require many of the available technologies to better emulate the way things happen in a traditional office setting."

Depending upon the particular job, most mobile and home office workers will need, at a minimum:

* high-speed Internet access
* a laptop computer (useful for working while your children are playing)
* printer, fax machine, copier, scanner (usually combined in one unit)
* power-surge protector
* backup system: external drive or online solution
* business telephone line with voice mail—which is frequently being replaced with a Unified Communications system using Voice Over Internet Protocol (VoIP).
* Some companies may also require additional equipment

for video conferencing, which is software to enable virtual meetings.

TELECOMMUTING ORGANIZATION LINKS

There are a number of national, regional, and local telecommunications organizations that may be able to assist you in terms of research for your proposal to work on a telecommuting basis. Here is a sampling of some of the key organizations:

* Canadian Telework Association: ivc.ca includes "the Canadian Scene" and the "U.S. Telework Scene." Be sure to follow the links to "Governments/Public Policy"
* Interagency Telework site, Federal Government: Telework. gov
* International Telework Association and Council: Working FromAnywhere.org
* Mid-Atlantic Telework Advisory Council, Washington, D.C.: M-ATAC.org
* The Telework Coalition: TELCOA.org
* Telework Exchange: TeleworkExchange.com

FURTHER INFORMATION ON TELECOMMUTING PROPOSALS

* Commuter Challenge, Telework Proposals: Commuter Challenge.org/cc/sample_docs.html
* Metropolitan Washington Council of Governments: "Telework Tips": MWCOG.org/commuter/teleworktips.html

Should You Consider Telecommuting?

Should you telecommute? There are many advantages and some disadvantages. For stay-at-home career moms, it can be an appealing work setup. Hey, who wants to wear a business suit and commute in snarling bumper-to-bumper traffic anyway? For some women, maybe even you, telecommuting might be a great short-term or long-term career strategy. Other women may want to work at home or outside the home on a more independent basis by starting their own business. Aspiring entrepreneurial moms can find out more in the next chapter.

5 BECOMING AN ENTREPRENEUR

"You have to have confidence in your ability, and then be tough enough to follow through."

—ROSALYNN CARTER, FORMER FIRST LADY OF
THE UNITED STATES (BORN IN 1927)

What do Lillian Vernon, Mary Kay cosmetics, and the Baby Einstein Company have in common? Each of these companies started as mom-run shoestring businesses. Lillian Vernon started her mail-order business with two thousand dollars in wedding-gift money. Today, the company ships 3.5 million products a year.

Mary Kay Ash (1915-2001) launched Mary Kay cosmetics in 1963 in a Dallas storefront with five thousand dollars and sold products door-to-door with nine salespeople. Today more than 1.5 million salespeople sell its products in thirty-two countries.

Julie Aigner-Clark started the Baby Einstein Company in order to give her child more exposure to the arts. Aigner-Clark and her husband invested eighteen thousand dollars in their first Baby Einstein video. According to some sources, the company's profit grew to ten million in 2000. Aigner-Clark reportedly sold the company to the Walt Disney Company in 2001.

Have you ever considered opening your own business? Maybe you will join this all-star group one day. Now may be the perfect time to start a business. Legions of women are starting both home-based and independent and franchised small businesses outside of the home. The direct party sales business is exploding in popularity as a way to earn cash.

By owning your own business, you'll be your own boss. You'll be able to set your own hours, greet your children when they get home from school, and have the satisfaction of creating your own career. It's not without risk, though. According to the U.S. Small Business Administration (SBA), nearly half of all small businesses fail within the first five years.

The key to a successful small business is going in with your eyes wide open. Thoroughly research all aspects of operating a small business in general as well your particular niche. While this process may seem overwhelming, it doesn't have to be. Free resources are available through the SBA and other government agencies as well as private organizations to help you get started. This chapter focuses on how to launch a small business—either a home-based business or a business located outside of the home.

Nearly 10.4 million companies across the United States are owned by women. Of these firms, 81 percent are self-owned and don't have any employees, for a total of 5.4 million firms, according to the Center for Women's Business Research. Of the nation's small businesses, 52 percent are operated from home and 2 percent are franchised, reported the SBA.

Do you want to join these 5.4 million women? There are many factors to consider before making the plunge into entrepreneurship.

The Upside to Small Business Ownership

On the positive side, operating a small business will give you a sense of independence, personal satisfaction, a more flexible lifestyle, and more time with your family. You can start your business as a part-time venture and increase your time and financial commitment if you are successful. Your profit, earnings, and growth potential are much higher than in a traditional job, and well, let's face it, new ventures are exciting—despite the risk.

Other advantages include:

- Eliminating the cost, time, and stress of commuting
- Control over your personal environment (temperature, light, getting a comfy chair, etc.)
- The end of office politics (need I say more?)

The Downside

Sigh . . . there's always a downside. There are many potential pitfalls to small business ownership. Chief among them is the risk of failure. But you can minimize this risk by planning your business carefully. Small businesses can fail for many reasons, including the location, inventory management, competition, credit arrangements, etc.—but many of these problems can be solved by being knowledgeable of all aspects of a business before you start. Successful business operation also takes chutzpah, hard work . . . and a little luck. You also need to be extremely self-disciplined and motivated.

Should You Start Your Business from Home?

Many stay-at-home career moms choose to run their business out of their own home. If you own a home-based business, you'll have lower start-up and operating costs. There are increased tax benefits by working at home. You'll have more independence in terms of your scheduling than working at another location. Your commuting time will be reduced to seconds.

You may save money on childcare if you're able to design a business that can be done with your children home and/or when they're in school or napping. It may be possible to get your whole family involved with your business. On the other hand, you may feel isolated when working at home.

Potential home business owners should be aware that many neighborhoods have deed restrictions preventing the operation of a home business. Check with your Home Owner's

Association (HOA) and your local government to find out about city or county home-business regulations. Even if a home business is allowable, your business activities may cause problems for you with your neighbors.

Getting the Family on Board

Having the support of your family is one of the most critical components for the success of a business. In order to strike a happy balance between family and work, you'll need to set up clear distinctions between "family time" and "work time."

Before starting a business, make sure you discuss it with your spouse and children. Discuss how home chores will be divided and how everyone will be affected. Make sure you get their input.

If you start a home-based business, rooms and space in your home may become cramped. Try to devise a way to limit the discomfort that this will cause your family, if possible. Some home-based business owners work out of a separate room (dining room, office, large closet, *whatever. . .*) Others prefer to sit at a desk in a common family area while their children play nearby. It depends on your own personality and your job. Some moms can work comfortably with plenty of distractions, while others need a quiet environment.

Depending on your business, it's usually preferable to get childcare during your working hours so you can focus your time and attention, especially if you interact with clients on the phone.

Should You Launch a Business with a Partner?

Some moms start a home business with a partner, usually another mom who lives in their community. This can be an excellent setup because the partners can share business expenses, plan the business together, and divide responsibilities based on each other's skills and scheduling concerns.

Jennifer Mangum and Suzan Meredith, for example, two Northern Virginia stay-at-home moms, teamed up to launch a home-decorating business called Redecorate Today in 2006. Together, they work about three days a week each, from 9 a.m. to 2 p.m.

"Suzan and I go to all our clients together, but one of us always takes the lead. By doing this, we can take on more clients than we could on our own," Mangum said. "I feel that we're more successful working together than if we worked independently. It's great to bounce creative ideas off of each other, and it helps to stick to our business plan and stay focused. I love having my own business and a business partner that shares the same excitement for decorating."

Marriage and Business—The Right Mix for You?

Some business owners launch businesses with their spouse. Careful consideration should be done before launching a family enterprise. It's important to determine if you can work side-by-side every day or if you would prefer to separate your personal and business life.

Other important questions to ask yourself and your spouse are:

- How will you handle disagreements about business?
- Can you separate business disagreements from your personal relationship?
- Can you divide tasks fairly according to your skills, experience, and interests?
- Can you both work as equal partners rather than one person trying to be the "boss"?
- Do you have a common goal and business vision?
- Can you afford for both of you to leave your jobs, if applicable, and start a business that may or may not be successful financially?

Self Assessment—The First Step to Entrepreneurship

It's important to assess whether you have the right type of personality for starting a business. You need to be self motivated and able to create your own highly structured work environment. Before starting your business, consider these key questions:

TWENTY QUESTIONS: IS SMALL BUSINESS OWNERSHIP
RIGHT FOR YOU?
Directions: Answer the following questions. If you answer "no" to any of the questions, carefully consider whether small business ownership is right for you.

1. Can you work independently without management to provide direction for you?
2. Can you work without personal interaction with colleagues?
3. Are you highly organized?
4. Can you make confident business decisions?
5. Do you have excellent research skills and the ability to learn the fundamentals and dynamics of small business ownership?
6. Can you interact effectively by e-mail and telephone?
7. Are you knowledgeable or have the ability and interest to learn about financial management?
8. Are you knowledgeable of computers and/or have a plan to get technical help, if needed?
9. Can you work alone without being "lonely"?
10. Can you define and enforce boundaries between your personal and business life?
11. Do you have excellent planning skills?
12. Do you have the patience and skills to deal with finances, inventory, schedules, and production, if applicable?
13. Can you deal effectively with demanding clients, unreliable vendors, etc.?
14. Are you assertive?
15. Are you competitive by nature?
16. Can you and your spouse deal with the stress of initial financial uncertainty?
17. Is your family on board with your decision to start a business?

18. Do you have the time needed to devote to your business?
19. Can you do this business when your children are in school or can you work effectively when they are at home? Or, can you find and afford reliable childcare when and if needed?
20. Do you have the motivation and passion to start and build this business at this time?

What Type of Business Should I Open?

Many stay-at-home career moms want to start a business, usually a home business, but don't know what type to start. If you're lucky, you may have the perfect business idea percolating in your mind. Otherwise, it's important to take the time to research possible businesses.

Many of the following ideas also apply to a business you could set up outside of the home, for example, a store or fitness studio. Franchising and direct sales will be discussed later in this chapter.

There are many possibilities for home-based careers in any of these categories. How do you find the best ideas? You can start by taking a self-inventory of your interests and passions. What do you love to do? Do you have a hobby that might transfer well into a career? What types of home businesses appeal to you now? Why? For example, do you love dogs? Gourmet food? Home decorating? Perhaps you can open a business related to your interests and passions.

Consider your professional skills. If you're a doctor, lawyer, accountant, computer programmer, writer, and so on, you may be able to set up an independent practice.

Have you considered becoming an eBay affiliate? You could join the more than 700,000 eBay businesses currently in operation. For more information, go to: pages.eBay.com/sellercentral/. Or have you considered setting up an Internet storefront to sell a product or line of products?

Are you creative? Have you invented something or could you invent something that might sell in the marketplace? Some moms have invented baby- and child-related items.

Can you think of a business that can solve an everyday problem? For example, you might start a business to help people in your community find babysitters or housecleaners. Or you might start an on-call secretarial service.

There are hundreds of home-business ideas—here's a sampling to help get you started:

- Accountant
- Artist
- Attorney
- Author
- Bed-and-Breakfast owner
- Bookkeeper
- Caterer
- Computer-repair specialist
- Daycare center operator
- Desktop publisher
- Event planner
- Financial planner
- Fitness instructor
- Graphic artist
- Importer/Exporter
- Internet retailer
- Inventor
- Limousine service
- Manufacturer: children's products
- Mortgage broker
- Office support specialist
- Photographer
- Private investigator
- Real estate appraiser
- Recruiter
- Researcher
- Software developer
- Technical writer
- Translator
- Travel agent
- Web designer

In a Mom's Own Words

Dorit Zeevi-Farrington, mom and owner of a New York Yacht Chartering Company

Dorit Zeevi-Farrington, a New York City mom, was enjoying a highly successful Wall Street career, but after having a baby, she decided to start a business that would enable her to have more time with her child. After considering several ideas, she decided to commission the building of a sixty-two-foot luxury yacht, and then with it launched Manhattan Steamboat Company, ManhattanSteamboat.com, a yacht chartering company in the New York City harbor. Now she cruises the harbor with her husband and "child on board"—a unique work-life balance solution.

"It truly was a difficult decision. On one hand, I had a fabulous job that paid handsomely. I was the head of an accomplished group that was highly appreciated within the company and had industry recognition. I traveled the world, stayed in the best hotels, and basically, was a type A-personality that follows the 'work-hard, play-hard' motto; I truly enjoyed my very-challenging job. But the truth is that I could not do it any longer. I had a baby at home and simply could not see a nanny raising her. I wanted to be involved with her upbringing from the very start. As the oldest of six girls, I knew that the early years are the most critical, and my decision to leave was primarily because of that. My daughter is now a six-year-old first grader. The outcome of my being with her all these years clearly shows."

Zeevi-Farrington said the genesis of this boating business was "a good collaboration between my husband and I: my husband's love of the water and my love of challenges, especially as related to building and growing new businesses. I always knew I would own my own business one day, but Wall Street made it easy for me to learn, to experience and also to leave. September 11 gave us both a new perspective on life and family."

(continued p.98)

(continued from p.97)

Despite having their own family business, it is still "challenging at times, especially in the summer" to achieve an optimal work-life balance in order to spend enough time with their daughter. "But, all in all, we wake up in the mornings together, we see her off to school, we pick her up in the afternoons, and we spend quality time together. That's just great for us."

In a Mom's Own Words
Lesley Spencer Pyle, mom and website owner

Lesley Spencer Pyle, a Texas mom of four children, owns several websites, including Home-Based Working Moms: HBWM.com, a professional association and online community for working parents. Pyle has been working at home for thirteen years.

"I have found working at home to be the ideal solution for balancing my career with my family. I don't feel like I have to sacrifice family time for my career or career time for my family. I am able to manage them both by working about six hours a day (when it works best for me) and creating a schedule that works best for me and my family. I absolutely love the freedom and flexibility that working from home allows.

"Having a family has given me a reason to think about what I truly want for my career, as well as what I'm not willing to sacrifice for my career. Family has had a good impact on my career because without it, I would not have the strong motivation and desire to help other women combine motherhood and career. I felt passionately about being at home with my firstborn, and I can relate to the desire many other moms feel who want to be at home at least part-time. Having a career has been positive for my family too. The additional income has eased the financial pressures, and my family enjoys being a part of some of my business discussions and decisions. It's exciting for them to see how my business has grown from the ground up.

"I decided to work from home after having my first child thirteen years ago. At the time, I was certain I would return to my full-time job and put my newly attained master's degree to good use by climbing the corporate ladder. However, motherhood had something else in store for me. The instant my daughter was born, I changed. My priorities changed. I could not imagine leaving her all day in someone else's care. I had to make some hard career decisions. I did, and I have never regretted it one bit. I love being a mom, and I love working from home."

Spotlight: Should You Open a Daycare?

For some moms, opening a daycare is a logical way to run a business and still have time for your children. Your children will play alongside the other children. You can't just put a sign up and set up shop, however. Every state has licensing requirements for daycare providers. To access the requirements for your state, visit the National Child Care Information Center (NCCIC) at NCCIC.org. Click on "State Contacts" then "State Child Care Licensing Agency," then the link for your own state. For a comprehensive overview on how to start a childcare business, go back to the home page: NCCIC.org, click on "For Providers," then "Child Care as a Business."

Spotlight: Wanna Go Global?

Have you ever thought about importing or exporting products to and from other countries? Perhaps you saw the perfect item to import to the United States on your last vacation. Or maybe you remember how you just could not find an item when you were in another country and think it might be a good product to export there.

Prospective entrepreneurs may want to set their sights abroad. If you're interested in starting an export or import company, check out the following websites:

- the International Trade Administration (ITA), Trade.gov; Trade.gov/ia/ for import information; Export.gov for export information.
- Links to more sites with international trade information can be accessed via the Federation of International Trade Associations, FITA.org, click on "Really Useful Links."
- Be sure to check out the SBA's online guide, "Breaking into the Trade Game—a Small Business Guide to Exporting." To access this article, go to SBA.gov, click on "About SBA," then "SBA programs," then "International Trade," then "Export Library," and then on the title of the article.
- For more information and networking opportunities, check out the Organization for Women in International Trade: OWIT.org.

Spotlight: Fitness Instructor

It's not that difficult to see how many moms end up leaping into fitness careers. They start fitness classes after the baby is born and sometimes just love it. Some moms have started fitness studios complete with babysitting facilities for both their clients and their own children. For links to information on certification programs for becoming an athletic trainer or a pilates or yoga instructor, etc., check out the U.S. Bureau of Labor Statistics webpage for "Fitness Workers" by accessing BLS.gov, and entering "Fitness Workers" into the search. Scroll down to the bottom of the page to find relevant links. Additional information can be found on JobMonkey.com/sports/, click on "Health & Fitness Careers."

Spotlight: Baby and Children's Products Businesses

Many moms get into retailing baby and children's products, either as an inventor, manufacturer, and/or online retailer. As a mom, you will have lots of ideas for products that you think would make your life a little easier. Read here about three moms who invented baby products and went on to form successful companies to market them.

Judy Pettersen, a Canadian mom, invented an infant carrier and started her own successful company to sell it. You probably saw Vin Diesel wearing her baby carrier, which she calls babyTrekker, in the Disney film, *The Pacifier*.

"I designed the babyTrekker baby carrier after my second daughter was born. I was frustrated with the carriers on the market and wanted one like the carrier I came up with," Petersen explained. Petersen had her "Eureka" moment when she realized that she had invented a viable product that she could sell to others. "After my friends saw and wanted one like the carrier I came up with, I started making them for other people. But it was on a family trip to Banff, Alberta, that I realized I had a potential business on my hands. Banff had a lot of international tourists, and I had people from other countries coming up to me and asking about the carrier. I was literally taking orders on the street!" she said.

Petersen went on to market the carrier at a home-business show and then set up a toll-free number to sell the product. Her sales rocketed. That was 1990. She worked out of her home office initially and eventually moved her office and shipping space into a separate facility. Her husband, mother, and five sisters helped with the business. Now her three daughters are grown up, and she continues to run her babyTrekker carrier business: babyTrekker.com.

Looking back, Petersen said, "It probably would have been a lot easier if I had continued as an unemployed stay-at-home mom. After all, I did it for seven years, and I loved it. But this opportunity called to me, and I really believed in it. It was a way of staying connected with my children, yet having an income of my own."

Jennifer Houghton, a South Berwick, Maine, mom of three children, started a children's hat manufacturing company "out of frustration with what was available." According to Houghton, "Honestly, the business started itself. I made a hat for my three month old . . . My girlfriend saw it and ordered six, and then showed her friend who has a local store. In just thirty days I had six wholesale accounts. By the end of the year, I had three women working with me, and we launched a website and our first retail location. I started this business with my first initial investment of $150 on a credit card."

Houghton started the hat business, theLittleHatCompany. com, in mid 2006. Two years later, she has sixteen employees at two store locations. According to Houghton, her first year revenue was about $10,000. In 2007, she had $107,000 in revenues.

Amy Long, a Texas mom of three boys and former register-ed nurse, invented a blanket that secures all the extraneous baby gear to a stroller, car seat, or baby carrier. She says she invented it because "necessity is the mother of invention!" and needed a secure blanket for her baby that would not fall off.

"I did not intend to invent something so I could start a business," Long said. "I needed a blanket that stayed on and made several for myself. As I used the blankets in public, requests from strangers became more frequent. I decided to make some extras to sell to friends and people in the community who inquired about my clip-on blanket. It soon became apparent that a demand existed for a blanket that stayed on. We created a website, Secure2me.com, and the buzz spread. Being entrepreneurs at heart, my husband and I made the decision to pursue the concept as a business, and Secure2Me, LLC, was incorporated in 2006."

"Eureka-I've Got it!" Have You Invented Something New?

If you have invented a new product, check out the following website for Mom Inventors, a site offering resources for entrepreneurial ventures, MomInventors.com.

Business-on-a-Shoestring Ideas

Starting a business doesn't always require a huge financial investment. Here are just a few business ideas for the "cash impaired" (i.e., most everybody):

- Cleaning service
- Computer repair
- eBay seller
- Family reunion planner
- Genealogy researcher
- Gift basket business
- Grant writer
- Home safety consultant
- Party planner
- Party supplier rental
- Personal trainer
- Pet sitter/dog walker
- Personal shopper
- Professional organizer
- Resume writer
- Seamstress

Group-Think Your Ideas

Do you love the idea of a group of like-minded women gathering to brainstorm your entrepreneurial ideas? If so, consider joining the Brain Exchange, theBrainExchange.com. In Brain Exchange meetings, women gather to ponder and brainstorm about many topics from relationships to career questions and entrepreneurial ideas.

Based in San Francisco, they have affiliate groups throughout the U.S. and in Mexico. If you can't find a local group, then you can start your own. Instructions are included on the website.

- Secretary on call
- Translator
- Tutor
- Website owner
- Wedding planner

Have an Idea? First Stop: SBA

While the process of starting and owning a business can seem intimidating from the outside, there are many free resources to help you investigate business ideas and learn how to set up and run a business.

First stop for perspective business owners is the U.S. Small Business Administration website, SBA.gov. Click on "Small Business Planner," which leads you to a comprehensive source of information on everything you need to know on how to plan, set up, finance, and manage a business. Be sure to check out the SBA's "Checklist for Starting a Business," a free, interactive tool for self-assessment to help you find out if your business idea might be viable.

To start, you may want to take some free online courses on how to set up, manage, and run a business. From the SBA homepage, click on "Services" and then "Online Training."

On this site, you can find information on how to write a business plan, which is a necessity for obtaining any needed financing. Very generally, a business plan is a written description of how you plan to establish and grow your business. It includes your marketing, financial, and management plans.

Interested business owners should also check out the resources for the SBA Office of Women's Business Ownership and Entrepreneurial Development. From the SBA.gov home page, click on "About SBA," then "SBA Programs," and then "Office of Women's Business Ownership." Here you'll find a wealth of information about small business and links to Women's Business Centers.

Business counseling assistance can be accessed via the SBA "Services" page. Here you will find a link to the Office of Small Business Development Centers (SBDC), which provides management assistance to current and prospective small business owners via branch locations throughout the United States. Click on "Association of SBDCs" to find an office in your regional area. You can also access America's Small Business Development Center Network at ASBDC-US.org. Enter your zip code in the search on the home page to find local SBDCs.

Another excellent resource for business counseling and information is the Service Corps of Retired Executives (SCORE), Score.org, which provides free online and face-to-face business counseling, mentoring, and training. Click on "Women" to find mentoring and services for women entrepreneurs.

Be sure to contact your state's business information center. These centers are set up to be a "one stop" gateway for information on how to start a business and obtain assistance from state government agencies. To find your state business information center, access your state's official site (example: Virginia.gov) and then find the link for "business" or "starting a business" on that home page.

Additional information about starting a business can be found at sites such as:

- Business gateway to the Federal Government, Business.gov
- Internal Revenue Service, IRS.com, click on "Businesses" then "Small Business & Self Employed One Stop Resource."

Financing Your Small Business

For information on financing your business, access SBA.gov, click on "Start Your Business" and then "Finance Start-up." Links to useful articles on this page include "Finding Capital" and "Federal Grant Resources." To start, check out "Financing Basics," which includes a discussion on the two types of business financing: "debt financing" and "equity financing."

Briefly, debt financing includes interest-bearing loans that need to be re-paid over a period of time. Equity financing means that investors help to finance a business in exchange for partial ownership of that business.

Sources for debt financing include banks, commercial finance companies, and the SBA. State and local governments have many programs to encourage small business. Check with your state or local government website. The most common source of financing for small business is personal loans from family, friends, colleagues, etc.

Commercial banks and related financial providers are the largest lenders of debt capital to start-up small businesses, providing 65 percent of the total traditional credit to small businesses in a recent year, the SBA reported.

While most small businesses use limited equity financing, as with debt financing, additional equity financing generally comes from loans from friends, family, former colleagues, etc. Other sources include financing from venture capitalists, which are "institutional risk takers" and may be a group of individual investors, government-assisted sources, or major financial institutions and "angel investors"—individuals seeking investment opportunities.

Additional sources of equity financing include the SBA-licensed Small Business Investment Companies (SBICs) and Minority Enterprise Small Business Investment companies (MSBIs).

In terms of home businesses, it's interesting to note that 28 percent of all entrepreneurs start their business without any capital at all, according to the U.S. Census Bureau. Nearly 10 percent of businesses are started by owners who used personal or business credit cards to finance the start-up. Credit cards account for much of the growth of small business during the past few years, according to the SBA.

Additional sources for information about financing a small business include:

- SCORE, Score.org, click on "Financing Your Business"
- Business.gov, click on "Small Business Guides" and "Finance"

Should You Open a Franchise?

You may want to consider buying a home-based or traditional store-front franchise business. You can pay a few thousand dollars or more than a million dollars. Franchises are one of the fastest-growing businesses in the United States.

Sampling of Women's Business Associations

- Alliance of Business Women International: ABWI.org
- American Business Women's Association: ABWA.org
- Association of Women Professionals: aWoman. org
- Business and Professional Women, USA: BPWUSA.org
- Digital Women: Digital-Women.com
- National Association of Women Business Owners: NAWBO.org
- National Association for Female Executives: NAFE.com
- National Women's Business Council: NWBC. gov
- US Women's Chamber of Commerce: USWomensChamber.com
- Women Entrepreneurs: WE-Inc.org
- Women's Business Enterprise National Council: WBENC.org
- Women-21.gov: comprehensive information on entrepreneurship

Franchising is a legal and commercial relationship between the owner of a business and their trademarks, i.e., a "franchisor" and an individual or group "the franchisee(s)" willing to buy into that business in a relationship similar to being a branch owner.

As with any business, there are pros and cons to owning a franchise. On the upside, you will buy into an established business that has brand recognition. You will not have to start a business from scratch. Generally speaking, franchises have a higher success rate than traditional businesses. Your franchisor will supply the marketing plans and business strategies.

On the flipside, as a franchisee your creativity will be limited. You will be contractually required to run the business in exactly the manner prescribed by the franchisee. You may be required to pay royalties and for equipment/supplies from your franchisor. The franchise will be for a fixed number of years. It may be difficult to sell the business down the line before the expiration of the franchise agreement because your franchisor may have to approve any future sale.

While we have all heard of the mega-franchises, from McDonalds to UPS stores, there are many home-based and small-investment franchise opportunities in a range of functions, for example:

- Bookkeeping
- Carpet cleaning
- Computer repair
- Cleaning
- Pet care
- Sales

If interested, your first stop for information should be the SBA website. At SBA.gov, click on "Small Business Planner," then "Start Your Business," then "Buy a Franchise." Here you'll find extensive information on how to buy a franchise. Be sure to check out the SBA's workbook: "Is Franchising for Me?"

Franchise counseling is available via the Small Business Development Center. (From SBA.gov, click on "About SBA," then "SBA programs," then "SBDC") and the Service Corps of Retired Executives (SCORE) at Score.org.

For additional information on starting and operating a franchise, check out the website for the American Franchisee Association: Franchisee.org.

Finding a Franchise

If you already have a business in mind, go directly to their website and click on "Franchise Opportunities." There are many free sites geared at finding a franchise. Be sure to check them out thoroughly to verify their legitimacy.

Franchise opportunities, including home-based, can be accessed via *Entrepreneur* magazine's "Franchise Zone": Entrepreneur.com/franchises/index.html.

How about Party Selling? The Suburban Craze

Chances are that you have attended at least one home sales party. There are parties for many types of products from Avon to Pampered Chef to Southern Living. Many stay-at-home career moms get into these businesses to earn some income, from a few hundred or few thousand per year to the equivalent of a full-time salary, depending on their goals and overall success.

In direct party sales, you sell products to your friends, neighbors, and their friends and neighbors, by having parties where you offer the products for sale. You may also sell the products through your website. These parties can be fun and give moms a great excuse to get out of the house and get together.

On the negative side, some of your neighbors may feel subtle, or obvious, pressure to buy products they don't want or need or can't afford. You, as the salesperson, may be uncomfortable hawking your products to your friends and neighbors. Or, on the other hand, you should have confidence in your product and feel you're providing a service by getting your product to your buyers, rather than having them have to buy something similar at the mall or grocery store.

Here's one caveat, some direct sales professionals feel obligated to go to all of their friends' and neighbors' sales parties. Some of the income they earn may go to buying other products from their neighbors. Is it worth it? Perhaps . . . if you love going to the parties and can still make a reasonable income for your own business, depending on your personal goals.

If you're interested in finding out more, check out the website for the Direct Selling Association at DSA.org. Here you'll find a wealth of information on direct selling and a directory of participating members. You can search the directory to find home business opportunities.

In a Mom's Own Words

Lisa Svendsen, Mom/Direct Sales Professional

Lisa Svendsen, a Virginia mother of three elementary-school-aged children, is an independent sales consultant for "Tastefully Simple," a party sales company that sells gourmet food through home taste-testing parties. When her first child was born, Lisa and her husband decided that she should stay home. But with two undergraduate degrees and a professional background as an accountant, Lisa wanted to find a way to parlay her professional background into starting a home business, which would allow her to make money on a schedule that would be "family friendly."

"I actually considered myself quite the home party snob before I began a career in direct sales myself. I thought that I had been to every party out there, until one time I was talking to my sister-in-law. She told me about a party she had attended called Tastefully Simple. When she told me it was just about *eating*, I was really surprised I had never heard of it before. I had been to direct sales parties where the focus was cooking, but never this. I was a stay-at-home mom with three kids under age four. I was intrigued, and something inside me said, 'I can do that.'

"I started my business when my three children were four months, two years, and three years old. I was home with my children when they were little, and I was able to celebrate all of their firsts with them—talking, walking, potty training, starting school. I have been able to volunteer in their classrooms and really get to know their teachers and classmates and chaperone field trips. I've been able to cheer them on at games, and celebrate their accomplishments and help them through their disappointments of the day.

"Now that my children are in elementary school, I have a significant additional amount of time during the day to spend on my business. Just like everyone else, I have to pay attention to use that time wisely so that when I pick my kids up from school, I can give them my undivided attention for a few hours. Routines help a lot. The key here is setting office hours. And I conduct my home parties in the evenings or on the weekends when my husband is here to watch the kids."

Beware of Home-Business Scams and Schemes

Unfortunately, many scammers target stay-at-home moms because of the huge demand for finding a home business. According to the Federal Trade Commission (FTC), an estimated 2.4 million people were victims of work-at-home schemes during the period of one recent year. It pays to do your homework and investigate business opportunities.

Be especially skeptical of business opportunities involving "envelope stuffing," "craft assembly," "medical billing," or any of the other business ideas that you may frequently receive in your spam filter or see announced on flyers plastered on poles around shopping centers. Why? Because these types of businesses are usually scams.

A number of organizations can help you avoids scams and schemes. Consult with the Better Business Bureau, BBB.org, to begin your research on a company or website. Be sure to also do your own "background search" on a company by searching for information on it via Google and other search engines.

Other excellent resources for investigating companies include:

- Consumer Affairs, ConsumerAffairs.com, click on "Scam Alerts"
- Internet Crime Complaint Center, IC3.gov, click on "Internet Crime Schemes"
- National Consumer League's Fraud Center, Fraud.org

Remember, there is no such thing as a "too good to be true" work-at-home business opportunity. Always ask for references if you are considering a business opportunity from an outside source. Be sure you report any scams that you unearth to the U.S. Federal Trade Commission, FTC.gov. So if it sounds "too good to be true," it probably is. Move on.

So, Should You Take Steps to Become an Entrepreneur?

Savvy stay-at-home career moms may want to consider starting their own business, buying into a franchise, or becoming a direct-sales representative. Entrepreneurial careers require extra effort, lots of creativity, a vision, and ingenuity. If you've got an idea, you may want to "run, not walk" to the U.S. Small Business Administration (SBA), Small Business Development Center (SBDC), and the Service Corps or Retired Executives (SCORE). These resources are free, comprehensive, and very easy to access. They are there to guide you toward your dreams. If you think small business ownership is for you, then—go for it, why not?

Help from Other Moms: Websites for Work-at-Home Moms

There are many mom-run websites that focus on starting and running a business from home. Here are just a few examples:

- Bizy Moms, BizyMoms.com
- Home-Based Working Moms, HBWM.com
- JobsforMoms.com
- Work at Home Moms, WAHM.com

6 SHORT-TERM SOLUTIONS FOR LONG-RANGE SUCCESS

"When one door of happiness closes, another opens; but often we look so long at the closed door that we do not see the one which has opened for us."
—Helen Keller, Author, Activist, and Lecturer, First Deaf-Blind Person to Graduate from College (1880–1968)

Many employees dream of becoming a "free agent"—quitting their job and peddling their skills as a consultant, independent contractor, or freelancer. As a stay-at-home career mom, now may be the perfect time to work as a free agent, whether you are presently working or are at home and thinking about re-starting your career. Some moms may dream of becoming a consultant or an independent contractor/freelancer. Others may want to consider other short-term options, including the possibility of working as a temp or substitute teacher. In all of these cases, you will be working on an ad-hoc basis, with the ability to determine the time that you want to devote to your job and whether you want to make a short-term or long-term commitment to it.

Short-term and contractual opportunities are plentiful in many regional areas. This can be advantageous to stay-at-home career moms. Many companies try to cut costs by hiring consultants. They may be looking for a specific expertise that you can offer.

Many stay-at-home career moms opt for temping positions. These types of jobs may lead to long-term employment. Benefits are sometimes included if you work a specified number of hours. While temp positions used to be limited to secretarial or administrative jobs, these days there are opportunities for accountants, computer specialists, editorial experts, and numerous other positions. There are even temp and contractual CEO positions.

Other stay-at-home career moms may want to consider substitute teaching. You will work the same hours as your children and have the flexibility to decline positions if you have other plans that day or week.

All of these short-term solutions offer you flexibility to determine your own schedule, while at the same time enabling you to continue your career and earn money.

If you're interested in working as a consultant or an independent contractor/freelancer, you are not alone. According to the U.S. Department of Labor, 8.5 million people presently work as consultants or freelancers.

As a consultant or an independent contractor, you are a hot commodity. Why? Companies can hire you without having to pay benefits. They also reduce their costs of recruiting and hiring a new employee. You will probably work out of your home, saving office space. Consultants and independent contractors are hired for a short-term or long-term job, so businesses don't have to incur the expense of keeping you on their payroll indefinitely.

While the terms "independent contractor" and "consultant" are sometimes used interchangeably, for the purposes of this chapter "independent contractor," also termed a "freelancer," is when you are hired to do one project at a time, for example, build a website, write a report, write a case study, modify a piece of software, etc. You may be re-hired for another project, but the contract is usually for one project at a time. While you may work from home or on-site, it's more typical to work from home.

As a consultant, you're hired to provide professional or expert advice to a business or individual. You typically work on a longer-term basis than an independent contractor and may work on a project with multiple components. Consultants are "independent contractors" since they work for themselves, so the distinction can be blurry. Generally speaking, however, independent contractors/freelancers tend to be hired because of their job function; for example, a company will hire a "writer" or "graphic designer," while consultants are hired to provide their expertise and advice. As an independent contractor, consultant, or freelancer, you are not employed by a company, but work for yourself.

For clarification purposes, note that it is also possible to work as a *management consultant* for a consulting organization, which is not the focus of this chapter. Management consultants work full time on a salaried basis and usually have an MBA. This chapter focuses on self-employment.

Short-Term Contractual Opportunities

If you're just stepping out of your workplace or are on good terms with your former employer, you may want to pursue contractual work with that company. As an independent contractor, you will work on a specific project for a set time frame. You may work on an hourly basis or per project.

By working as an independent contractor, you will be able to "stay in the game" and keep your name known in your place of business and industry as a whole. It will enable you to maintain your skills and have the ability to pick and choose the projects that suit your career goals and scheduling limitations. You will keep your contacts current and your resume up-to-date.

Job insecurity is the greatest disadvantage of working as an independent contractor. An independent contractor needs to constantly hustle for new projects. If you are well connected in your industry, then you may be able to market yourself easily. If you are not, then you may have to spend a significant amount of time marketing your services.

Independent contractors do not receive company benefits, but may be able to charge more than you would have received as an employee. This may be acceptable to some moms whose spouse has insurance coverage through their employer. On the other hand, it's important to consider and project the cost of lost retirement savings.

Sampling of Independent Contractor/Freelancer Specialties

- Accounting/bookkeeping
- Computer programming
- Editing/proofreading
- Event/party/wedding planning
- Financial planning
- Floral designing
- Fundraising
- Grant writing
- Photography
- Professional organizing
- Resume writing
- Translating
- Tutoring
- Web designing
- Writing

Finding Contract Positions

If you're interested in pursuing opportunities with other companies/organizations or are seeking contracts in a new career field, you will need to market your services directly to prospective clients and/or apply to job postings on the Internet.

As a first step—identify the skills and qualifications that you need to be competitive. For example, if you want to obtain freelance writing jobs, you will need writing skills and experience. If you are looking for administrative jobs, are you proficient with word processing, PowerPoint, and Excel? If you want to do contract landscape work, do you have the skills, experience, and equipment?

You may find that you will need additional training or coursework, certifications, and/or licenses. If you are up-to-date with your expertise, you will need to do some strategic thinking and competitor research on how to place yourself in the marketplace. Chances are that you will need to focus on a niche area of business, for example, instead of offering general web design services, you might want to offer web design services to nonprofit organizations in a particular field or train people on how to design and maintain websites.

To start, you can advertise your services by word of mouth to friends, colleagues, and people in your network. Be sure to join one or two relevant trade organizations and consider joining local civic organizations where you can network, for example, your local Chamber of Commerce or Rotary Club.

Consider advertising your services in local papers, flyers on bulletin boards, etc. Design a brochure, business cards, and business stationery. Launch a website to effectively market your services.

Independent contractor and freelance opportunities can be found via advertisements on Internet job boards, including CareerBuilder.com, Monster.com, and others. CraigsList.com often includes short-term independent contract and freelance opportunities.

You can also find and compete for short-term gigs through specialized sites, such as Aquent.com, Elance.com, Guru. com, and SoloGig.com. Many of these types of sites charge a registration and/or membership fee and receive a percentage of the pay you receive from jobs obtained via their site. The advantage to using these services is that you can find jobs without having to cultivate your own client base. On the flip side, however, the agency will deduct a commission, and you will be earning less than you would by finding your own opportunities.

Becoming a Consultant

Stay-at-home career moms with professional experience may want to market their expertise as a consultant. As a consultant, you market yourself as an expert in a specific field. You provide advice, analyze and solve problems, and make recommendations to a client. You may be hired as a catalyst for change and as a source of objectivity for problem solving. Consultants may work as teachers/trainers to full-time employees in an organization. Or you may provide specialized work, for example, writing, website design, programming, etc.

A consultancy is a small business and prospective consultants should refer to Chapter Five for the specifics of starting a small business. Consultants can work on a part-time or full-time basis and generally start and/or continue to run their business from home. Some consultants may work on-site at a company for a short period of time and may be hired to supplement staff.

Do You Have the Right Qualifications?

While it may seem that everyone calls himself or herself a consultant, it's important to assess if you have the needed qualifications in order to market yourself effectively. If you have substantial industry experience and/or special skills, you may already be well aware of your qualifications and potential markets for your expertise.

Other considerations include assessing your personal skills—organizational skills, time management, sales, etc., and ability to network and constantly drum up new business. As with any business, carefully consider if you have the right temperament to run it.

Twenty Questions: Do You Have the Skills to Be a Consultant?

Directions: Answer each of the following questions. If your answer is "no," carefully consider whether becoming a consultant is the best career choice for you.

1.   Are you an expert or do you have substantial experience in an industry or topic?
2.   Is your expertise in high demand?
3.   If you do not have the requisite expertise, can you get it by taking courses, obtaining certifications, etc.?
4.   Can you identify problems and are you a problem solver?
5.   Are you a strategic thinker?
6.   Can you work independently without supervision?
7.   Are you content when working alone?
8.   Are you creative and do you like coming up with new ideas and ways of doing things?
9.   Are you a confident negotiator?
10. Are you highly organized?
11. Can you market yourself and constantly seek out new clients?
12. Are you well connected in your industry or do you have the ability and patience to cultivate a network?
13. Do you have excellent interpersonal skills?
14. Do you have excellent writing skills?
15. Are you good at doing research on your competitors?
16. Are you able to diligently keep up with developments in your industry?
17. Do you have the ability to weather financial "down times" in your business, financially and emotionally?
18. Is your family on board with your decision to transition to consulting?
19. If you are employed, can you afford the loss of benefits?
20. Are you willing to "bet the farm?" In other words, start your consulting business, knowing full well that it may or may not be financially and professionally successful?

Consulting Fields

Consultants can specialize in anything from how to create a more environmentally friendly company to how to upgrade the company's IT systems, from how to improve a company's public image to how to invest its capital—and everything in between. Two of the largest growing consulting fields are computer-related or IT consulting and all facets of business consulting, from human resources to productivity and efficiency improvement to strategic planning, mergers and acquisitions, and more.

Many consultants specialize in a particular field where they already have substantial expertise. Others develop or improve their core knowledge in a niche before starting a consulting business in that field.

Sampling of Consulting Business Fields

- Accounting/bookkeeping
- Advertising/marketing
- Business analysis
- Career coaching
- Communications/writing/editing
- Computer/IT
- Engineering
- Environmental
- Executive search
- Finance
- Fundraising
- Grant writing
- Human resources
- Management
- Manufacturing
- Organizational development
- Political consultant
- Public relations
- Real estate
- Sales and business development
- Taxes
- Training
- Workplace safety

How to Start a Consulting Business

Most consultants start their business as a sole proprietorship

In a Mom's Own Words
Lori Ermi, Mom and Maryland-based Consultant

Lori Ermi, mom of a toddler and step-mom to a teenager, started the Ermi Group, LLC, a human capital and executive coaching firm, after working in the corporate realm for twenty-two years. While serving in one of the HR leadership roles she's held, she attended a six-month certificate program in Leadership and Coaching at Georgetown University as an investment in her development. After being laid off for the third time in six years, Ermi had the contacts and the confidence to go out on her own, in large part due to her Georgetown experience.

"I declared my intention to adopt a baby during my journey at Georgetown and had joint-custody of my then thirteen year-old step-daughter," Ermi explained. "I worked full time (sixty plus hours a week plus three-hour commutes each day) for almost a year after getting Kate as a newborn in 2006."

Even though Ermi's husband is a full-time, stay-at-home dad, she craved more time with her baby. "Sometimes I didn't even see her before I left for work each day if she was still sleeping," Ermi said. After starting her own business, Ermi said that she now gets to spend much more time with her child. "I get to feed her breakfast and lunch at least two to three times per week and am home before 6:00 p.m., or earlier, after previously getting home at 7:00 or 8:00 p.m. and basically putting her to bed. I also protect one morning each week to attend Kindermusik [a 'mom and me' music program] with her. I just tell my clients I have another commitment and no one seems to flinch!"

Ermi has transformed the family's finished basement into an office suite and works part of the week out of her home. If her husband has to run an errand then her baby plays downstairs alongside her while she works.

"I love my new role. What a deal!" Ermi said.

from home—a setup that may be particularly appealing to you. Many consultants receive a high compensation, depending on their expertise, but usually don't start making money until their business is well established.

As a mom, you may be thinking: "How could I fit this business in while caring for my children?" At first, you will probably need to conduct your business while your children are sleeping, during naptimes, play dates, etc. Start small. You will have more time when your children are in school full time. If your consulting business takes off right away, then you can consider hiring childcare.

To start your business, review the fundamentals of how to start a small business in Chapter Five. With this in mind, choose your field. You probably have a good idea of what type of consultant work you are qualified to do, but if not, be sure to take the time to research all possibilities, based on your background, education, and skills. Strategize how you want to position yourself in the consulting field and how wide or narrow of a niche you will pursue. Research your potential competitors. Can you think of a new or better niche area to specialize in? Is the market already saturated for a certain type of consultant? Is there a great need for your type of consulting in your community, industry, the nation, the world? Can *you* fill that need?

Next, build your credentials. If you cannot position yourself as an instant expert, take some time to build your credentials. You may need additional training or to take a course or two to get back up to speed with your industry. A certification may be required or recommended to have credibility in a particular field. Check with relevant industry and trade associations.

You can also start to market yourself and your expertise by writing articles, giving speeches and presentations, and getting your name known or "re-known"—if you have been out of an industry for a while. At this point, you may want to focus on creating a web presence by writing a relevant blog, launching a website, and joining in on relevant online discussions on industry sites and using your own name as the signature after your remarks. Build your network by joining relevant industry organizations.

To find your clients, use word-of-mouth and targeted advertising in appropriate publications. Create a brochure. Focus on establishing your web presence and be sure to link your site to other relevant sites. Continue to build your network and spread the word about your new consultancy. Consider volunteering your services to get yourself started. Take some time—consulting businesses tend to start slowly, client by client. You may find that you eventually need to turn clients away. Be sure to track developments in your industry and adapt your business as needed. Consulting can be extremely rewarding— both professionally and in terms of financial compensation— but it's not for the "risk-intolerant" and those who prefer an easier lifestyle and a steadier paycheck.

As with any small business, your next step will be to create a business and marketing plan. Since you will be selling your own expertise, you can probably start your business without any significant start-up costs. Your compensation structure can be determined by researching your industry and competitors. It is advisable to have a lawyer review your contracts. As a small business owner, you will compute your own taxes and social security. Consult SBA.gov and IRS.gov for detailed information.

The Ins and Outs of Temping

For some stay-at-home career moms, being a freelancer or a consultant may be the ultimate challenge—others may prefer a more laid-back approach to short-term employment and may want to work for a temporary agency as an on-call secretary or administrator. Temp opportunities are also available in job functions as diverse as accounting, editing, paralegal work, and more. Temps can work on a day-by-day basis or on a longer contract basis. More than three million people per day are working on a temporary basis using staffing companies, according to the American Staffing Association (ASA).

In a Mom's Own Words
Debra Haas, Mom and Texas-based Consultant

Debra Haas, an Austin, Texas, mom, started her own consulting business, Haas Policy Consulting, HaasPolicy.com, in order to achieve a better work-life balance as a mother. She also teaches courses at the University of Texas.

Haas runs a one-women firm specializing in public finance and program valuation focused on, but not entirely limited to, public education issues. Her clients include school boards, teacher organizations, state government, political consulting firms, and not-for-profit organizations.

"After my daughter was born I was the first woman on the professional staff at the Legislative Budget Board to go on a part-time schedule. I had very supportive management, but my life reached a point that demanded more flexibility. I am a classic member of the 'sandwich' generation.

"I had a young daughter, two school-aged stepsons who would spend two to four weeks at a time with us, and my mother, who lived in another state, was battling a very aggressive form of cancer. By leaving the traditional workplace and going out on my own, I was able to take my daughter, who was not yet in school, and spend extended periods of time visiting my parents when my mom was healthy enough to be around small children. In the four and a half years between going out on my own, and my mother's death, we spent a lot time together.

"I knew I couldn't devote the time to my staff and state job I needed to if I was going to give my daughter the opportunity to spend a lot of time with her grandmother— so the choice seemed pretty obvious. It was made much easier because my husband was incredibly supportive of the decision and has always had a job with benefits. It also helped that I was established in my profession and knew people who were willing and able to help me get early work.

"The flexibility also meant that when my stepsons came to visit, we could have them here for longer periods of time because I could make my schedule work around theirs. Otherwise, the visits would have been shorter, or we would have been required to find care for them when they were here.

"Having the business helps my whole family. I certainly could have gone back to a more traditional job—and had offers—once my daughter started public school and after my mom died. The first year after my mom's death, I went home to help my dad a lot—about once every six weeks, something I would not have been able to do if I had gone back to the traditional work place.

"By having this business—and the ability to set my own schedule, I have been able to continue my professional life, which is very important to me, while having the benefits of being a stay-at-home mom. I have been very involved in my daughter's school and after school activities, I am a Girl Scout leader, I'm home to help with homework, and now that she is in middle school, I don't worry about what she is doing, or who she is with in the afternoons, because I am with her."

By working as a temp, you will have the freedom to designate the days that you are available and the ability to accept or decline specific jobs. In many cases, you may be required to work full time during business hours, so you may have to find a sitter for when your children arrive home from school if you are planning to work in an office. Other moms with marketable skills have negotiated part-time temp assignments. According to the ASA, 79 percent of staffing employees work full time during regular business hours.

Temping is a great way to bridge back into the workforce. It gives you an opportunity to meet people, network, and showcase your skills to employers. You will be able to update your resume and obtain up-to-date references. By working on a temporary basis, you will be able to find out if that company would be a good fit for you. According to the ASA, twelve million employees nationwide were hired initially as temps.

Many staffing companies provide free professional office and computer training to employees, a good way to get your skills up-to-date. Some companies provide health insurance, vacation pay, and retirement plans.

If you're interested in temping, access the website for the American Staffing Association, AmericanStaffing.net. To find a staffing company in your area, click on "Job Seekers," and then "Find a Staffing Company." You can search staffing companies near your zip code and designate the types of jobs you are seeking by the following categories: Health Care, Office Clerical, Technical, IT, Industrial, and Professional/Managerial.

For more information about temporary staffing, check out sites such as Net-temps, an online staffing site, Net-Temps. com. Net-temps is a job board for temporary and full-time employment. Jobs are posted on this site by staffing companies, not employers. You can click on "Find a Staffing Agency" to find agencies in your area.

If you're interested in a specific employment niche, for example, legal temping, IT temping, etc., use any search engine and designate that term and "staffing agency." Examples of industry specific temp agencies include: Accountemps.com, and iCreatives.com, for temp graphic designers.

Another search method is to access SimplyHired.com or CraigsList.com and designate "temporary" as your search term. It is possible to save your search and have new jobs that match your terms e-mailed to you on a regular basis.

Seasonal Work

To get seasonal work, you don't necessarily have to don a Mrs. Santa suit (although it might be fun!), but opportunities abound, especially in retail, during the holiday season. Realistically, however, this is when your children are home from school and perhaps the least likely time for you to want to seek employment. Some moms, however, like to work at their favorite retail store during the pre-holiday rush and get the store discount while their spouse watches the children.

You could also work during summer break in a "mom-friendly" job; for example, you might work at a camp or daycare center during the summer if you are able to bring your children with you to work.

Stay-at-home career moms with a tax background may want to consider seasonal tax employment. There are many opportunities in this bourgeoning field, whether working directly for a company or selling your services as an independent contractor. Seasonal tax preparers can work on-site or out of their home office.

Reverse Seasonal Work

If you're interested in retail sales, you might consider reverse seasonal work. In this setup, you work while college students are away at school. You are off when they are back, i.e., winter break, spring break, and the summer. Keep in mind that your children's school holidays might not coincide neatly with your college-student counterpart. The key is to seek employment with a retailer who will be flexible, and well, needs you because of the general shortage of workers in the retail industry.

Is Mystery Shopping for Real?

Some of us can only dream of being paid to shop while piling packages on our strollers while we go to the mall with our children. Is it for real? There are legitimate mystery shopping opportunities, but be aware that the Internet is littered with mystery shopping scams. The pay is generally low and job assignments can be sporadic. That said, the job could be fun and give you a little extra cash. Hey, you're at the mall anyway, right? For more information, consult the website for the Mystery Shopping Providers Association, MysteryShop.org. Job listings can be found by clicking on "North America" and "Shoppers."

Substitute Teaching

As a mom, you probably volunteer at your child's school and

wonder if you should consider substitute teaching. Most school systems face acute shortages of qualified subs and would welcome your application. Subbing is an excellent job for many moms because you work during school hours and have the flexibility to turn down jobs. Some moms go into subbing, love it, and end up making a career change to teaching. Information on teaching careers can be found in Chapter Nine.

It's not necessary to have teaching credentials in order to become a sub. Most districts require a high school degree; some districts require an undergraduate degree from a university. Applicants will be given a thorough background check and may be tested on basic skills and if they have a personality suitable to teaching. Successful applicants will attend some type of training session and may be required to participate in yearly refresher courses.

Substitute teachers are hired on the district level. To find out more about substituting in a particular district, access the home page for the National Center for Educational Statistics, NCES.ed.gov, and click on "Search for Schools." If you are interested in subbing in a private school, contact that school directly.

Does a Short-Term Solution Work for You?

Some stay-at-home career moms welcome the flexibility of obtaining a short-term solution, whether as an independent contractor/freelancer, consultant, temporary staff worker, seasonal employee, or substitute teacher. Many of these jobs can be used as a springboard to transition back into the workplace as a full-time employee. On the other hand, some moms work for years on a temp, freelance, or contract basis and love the flexibility that it gives them and their family. The caveat in all of these positions is that there is no guarantee of steady work. Undoubtedly, there will be dry spells when you do not get any calls to work. Other times you may be turning work away. Despite that uncertainty, for some moms, short-term employment is the perfect setup while balancing raising their children and pursuing their career.

PART III

Transitioning Back to the Workplace

7 IS IT TIME TO GO BACK TO WORK FULL TIME?

"The winner of the hoop race will be the first to realize her dream, not society's dream, her own personal dream."
—BARBARA BUSH, FORMER FIRST LADY OF
THE UNITED STATES (BORN IN 1925)

Should you go back to work full time? It's a big decision, and timing is essential. You may want or need to go back to work at some point. If you've kept up with your networking and your skills as a stay-at-home career mom, you'll always have the option to jump back into your career.

Important considerations include how to achieve an optimal work-life balance. Flextime and flexible scheduling are becoming increasingly accepted norms in many industries. With careful research, you may be able to find professional opportunities in "family friendly" companies.

When making your decision, you'll need to carefully consider your professional, financial, and personal priorities and needs. Factors to consider include the costs and emotional aspects of childcare for both you and your children.

Despite media frenzy and highly vocal partisans on the merits of working full time or staying at home, there is no *right* or *wrong* decision. Only you can determine what's right for you and your family.

Professional Considerations

Let's face it. Some women are just plain bored when at home. They miss the workplace and working part-time is not enough for them. They don't have any entrepreneurial aspirations, so they're not planning to start their own business.

Or they don't have the money needed to start a business, or they're uncomfortable with the unpredictable income that's part of owning a business. These moms may prefer to work in an office environment and may enjoy the challenge of climbing the corporate ladder. These moms usually worked hard to obtain the position they had before leaving to stay home with children. They usually loved their job and continue to be ambitious. Basically, they long for the excitement of the workplace.

If you're this type of mom, then you may love staying home with your children, but always feel like something is just "missing." You may be so involved with volunteer activities that you're working full time anyway—and not for pay—and end up leaving your children with sitters or neighbors on a regular basis. Or, your children may be in school full time and you find yourself to be who you never imagined—a housewife. Your days consist of cleaning the house and getting your nails done. You stayed home to raise your children, not clean the house and primp your nails, and are now ready to "get a life."

If this is your situation, then you should consider whether you should go back to work full time. It's not good for you or your children if they know that you would rather be working, whatever their ages. And don't think you can hide it—children are very perceptive.

Financial Considerations

For many stay-at-home career moms, financial considerations loom as a high priority. But can you afford to go back to work? As Ralph Waldo Emerson once said, "Money often costs too much." Daycare is expensive—typically ranging from $4,000 to $10,000 per year for each of your children. It's critical to carefully calculate the costs of childcare for before and after school, summer vacation, spring break, teacher's work days, and other holidays.

If you go back to work full time, you'll also need to factor in commuting expenses (gasoline, car maintenance, tolls, and/ or public transportation), professional clothing, lunches, and more. Depending on your projected salary, you may still be able to earn an income that makes it financially beneficial—or not. You should consider all projected expenses and do a cost-benefit analysis in terms of your expected salary. And check with a tax professional if you think your added salary might hurl you and your spouse's combined incomes into a new tax bracket.

You may find that your expenses will trump your potential earnings, but remember to take your long-term projected income into account. In other words, if you accept X salary now, then it may lead to a better job with a higher salary down the line. And, if you want to work, despite the costs of going back to work, remember that daycare is a "shared expense"—in other words, both you and your spouse are jointly responsible for paying for it. If you add your salaries together and deduct the daycare expenses from your joint income (not just yours), then you may find that going back to work is financially beneficial.

Some stay-at-home career moms go back to work for the benefits, especially retirement benefits. Many moms go back to work to start saving for their children's college tuition and expenses.

If you have become recently divorced or widowed, then you may need to find full-time employment, all these considerations aside. You may now be in a position where you need and want to re-enter the full-time career workforce.

Some moms also desire not to have the financial dependence that they may feel if they aren't working at all or earning what they feel is enough money by working part-time, telecommuting, or running their own business.

Other stay-at-home career moms find that they are tired of scrimping and cutting costs. Their children may be older now, and they may be ready to get a bigger paycheck. Perhaps they want to work to move to a better neighborhood or pay for private school for their children. Or, they may want more luxuries for the family, for example, money for vacations.

Personal Factors

Personal and emotional factors may be your most difficult considerations. If you have been fortunate enough to stay home, how will you and your child/children handle it if you are working full time? Are you okay with leaving them in daycare or with a sitter after school? What about during the summer? Do you really want to leave them in back-to-back day camps? And we have all been to school functions where parents were invited and one or two children sat alone because their parents couldn't make it. Other parents and the teacher always try to cheer them up and get them involved in the activity at their table, but the fact is that you can always tell that they know that their own parent is not there. Children do not understand inflexible bosses and pressing deadlines.

If you go back to work, family routines will need to change. You and your spouse will have to divvy up responsibilities even more equitably. You need to ensure that you are not stuck with the "second shift" of doing all the housework after working all day while your spouse lounges on the couch. What type of schedule will you set up to equitably divide household chores and responsibilities?

As a couple, you'll need to decide who will stay home on snow days or days when your child is sick and who will take off time for doctor's appointments. What happens if one of you needs to stay home to wait for a repairman? And what if you're both running late coming home from work? How will you arrange back-up childcare? What if your child needs to go home sick during the day?

As parents, you will need to come up with a plan for enabling your children and yourselves to continue to have quality time together as a family. Family will always need to be your priority. You and your spouse may need to give up your own personal hobbies for now in order to fit it all in. While you'll be tired after a long work day, you and your spouse's first priority after getting home from work will be helping your child or children with their homework. Chores like grocery shopping, cleaning, and bill paying may need to be done together as a team at odd hours and during the weekend when you would both rather be relaxing with the family.

And ideally, you and your spouse will make attending school events and activities a priority. You and your spouse can alternate attending these activities so that one of you is always there, to the extent possible.

As a full-time employee, you may feel "time deprived." Sixty-seven percent of employed persons, both women and men, say they don't have enough time with their children, 63 percent say they don't have enough time for their spouse, and more than half of full-time employees say they don't have enough time for themselves, according to a Family and Work Institute study. Since 78 percent of couples are currently dual earners according to recent statistics, home life has become increasingly hectic.

Adding to this strain is the number of hours that most professional employees work each week. According to the Sloan Work and Family Research Network at Boston College, nearly 20 percent of employees work an average or forty-nine hours or more. A typical dual-earner couple works ninety-one hours a week combined—which doesn't leave a lot of time for their families.

But while balancing your work and home commitments and priorities may seem overwhelming, you *can* make it work for you, especially, or perhaps even *only*, if you work for an employer that values work-life balance and flexibility with its employees.

Work-Life Balance

America's workplace is changing. Twenty years ago, it was acceptable, even admirable, to some, to work in a cutthroat, high-pressure environment. Overtime was expected and those who left early for family reasons were seen by some as shirking their professional responsibilities. Professional moms wore female versions of men's power suits, with little floppy bows at their neck instead of a tie, and tried to prove they could keep pace in the rat race. Their family and personal lives may have suffered, but back then, it was part of the ticket for success.

Fast-forward . . . an increasing number of women (and men) are demanding—and getting—jobs with more acceptable work-life balance. America's workplace culture is changing. An increasing number or organizations and companies are promoting flexible work-life policies, including:

* Part-time and job-sharing opportunities (see Chapter Three)
* Telecommuting options (see Chapter Four)
* Flexible hours for full-time employees
* On-site or subsidized childcare
* Leaves of absence or sabbaticals

Flextime

According to a recent study, nearly one-third of companies offer flexible scheduling. Workplace flexibility means that an employee has a higher degree of control over their own schedule and the hours that they work, within set parameters.

In a flexible scheduling setup, you work a set number of hours, but not during the nine-to-five traditional time bracket. You may start very early, or later in the day, and then work the same number of hours. A stay-at-home mom may be able to set up a job that allows her to work from seven to three, for example, enabling her to go home at the end of her children's school day. Some employers allow employees to vary their schedules by day, week, or month, so that you can plan in advance to attend functions at your children's schools, take them to the physician, etc., without being penalized financially or professionally.

Other types of flextime schedules may involve working on a condensed schedule, for example, working four ten-hour days a week—enabling you to have a three-day weekend, every weekend. Or, for example, you might work shorter days in a six-day week.

Many employers offer a combination of work-life benefits, including flexible scheduling and the opportunity to work some or all of the time on a telecommuting basis and/or part-time basis.

Employee-Sponsored Childcare

On-site daycare is offered in only about 5 percent of companies nationwide, according to a study by the Society for Human Resource Management. Many of these companies are among the nation's largest companies.

To read about some of the companies that offer on-site daycare, go to *Working Mother* magazine's "100 Best Companies," of which 53 percent offer on-site daycare: WorkingMother.com/web?service=vpage/1046

Extended Leaves of Absence

Some companies offer paid or unpaid extended leaves of absence or sabbaticals for new moms beyond the twelve weeks of unpaid family leave required for qualifying companies under the Family and Medical Leave Act (FMLA). Others offer full pay for a set number of weeks within the twelve weeks. Some companies have programs in place so that new moms can ease back in to working full time gradually by working part-time and/or telecommuting for a set period of time after their full-time maternity leave has ended.

Several companies offer extensive leaves of absences to new moms. At both Deloitte & Touche USA, LLP, and Price-waterhouse-Coopers, LLP, for example, moms can take off up to five years before returning to work. Similar programs exist at both companies to help keep these employees up-to-date during their time at home—including opportunities such as classes/training, networking opportunities, career coaching, and the possibility of taking on short-term assignments.

IBM Corp. allows new moms six weeks of paid time off, with the option of extending their leave to three years. Several companies offer a year of unpaid leave, including Johnson & Johnson and Eli Lilly & Co.

In a Mom's Own Words
Elizabeth Ruben, On-Site Daycare Fan

Elizabeth Ruben, a Durham, NC, mom has the highest accolades for the on-site daycare facilities offered by SAS, Inc., a Cary, NC, corporation. Ruben was employed by SAS while two of her sons attended the on-site Montessori school.

"My two sons were enrolled in the SAS on-site daycare facility from three months of age until they entered kindergarten. For our family, the SAS Montessori daycare and preschool has been an amazing opportunity.

"The daycare is—literally—across the street from my office. If my child is sick, for example, if he has an ear infection, I can call the health center, make an appointment quickly, then walk across the street, pick up my child and walk him the 200 yards, or so, to the healthcare center. Typically, I'm back at my desk in an hour and can get back to my work. I don't lose too much work time, or momentum in my work. If my child was in an off-site daycare, I would have to drive there, pick him up, drive to the doctor's office, wait, and then drive back. It would probably take me several hours or even a half-day. That's a significant amount of time carved out of my day."

Ruben said that the on-site daycare "absolutely" factored into her decision to keep working full time after her first child was born. "For one, the subsidized childcare makes it financially feasible to go back to work. Also, being so close to my children, being able to be there quickly for them when needed makes a huge difference. Last, knowing that they are so incredibly well-cared for—I can relax and focus on my job."

More Parental Perks

According to the Polling Company/WomanTrend, the trend nationwide is that companies are offering an increasing number of benefits for parents, including:

- networking opportunities for working parents
- private lactation rooms
- consultants for pregnancy-related issues
- assistance researching childcare options

First Step to Finding a Flexible Job

Many, but not all, companies are finding ways to promote a better quality of life for employees. To find out if a company is "family friendly" in terms of your own priorities, check out their website and see if they have posted information about their work-life policies and procedures.

As a prospective employee, you can also contact the company's human resources office to ask them for brief information about the company's general work-life policies, including the possibility of working on a flexible schedule, telecommuting, working part-time, etc. They may or may not be amenable to talking to you about their policies, but it is worth a try.

If you're serious about applying to work at a company, then you may want to contact an employee at that company to request an informational interview to ask their opinion on their company's work-life policies and procedures.

Researching Flex Policies Online

Working Mother magazine's annual "Best Company" rankings is an excellent source of information for finding flexible jobs. To access the site, go to WorkingMother.com and click on "Best Companies" and "100 Best Companies." Here you can find out about which of the magazine's top 100 picks for working women offer flextime scheduling, telecommuting, job sharing, part-time positions, etc. The listings also note whether the company offers on-site or subsidized childcare, and if the company offers backup childcare. Many of the included companies offer adoption assistance. Other perks are noted as well—for example, whether a company operates or sponsors summer camps for children. Companies are included that offer health insurance to part-time employees.

Fortune magazine posts an annual list of "100 Best Places to Work." To access the site, go to Money.cnn.com and click on "100 Best Companies to Work for."

Additional information on family-friendly companies can be found by accessing the site for the Families and Work Institute, a nonprofit research organization, FamiliesAndWork.org. From the homepage, download the following report: "Making Work 'Work': New Ideas from the Winners of the Alfred P. Sloan Awards for Business Excellence in Workplace Flexibility" to find detailed information about many family-friendly companies nationwide.

Small Companies May Be Your Answer

Depending on your career goals, don't ignore smaller companies and nonprofit organizations when scouting out flexible work opportunities. While there are many work-life opportunities at the corporate giants, remember that opportunities may also exist in small companies. To find a list of some of the country's best small- and medium-size companies, access this site:

- Great Places to Work, Best Small and Medium Companies in America: SHRM.org/bestcompanies

Flexible Staffing Agencies

A growing number of staffing agencies focus on helping their clients obtain jobs with flexible schedules, primarily contract and consulting positions, as well as part-time and telecommuting jobs. Staffing agencies that focus on placing moms in flexible jobs are located in many locations across the country. To find out some examples, go to page 189 in Chapter Ten.

In a Mom's Own Words
Amy Cropper, Mom & Flextime Professional

Amy Cropper, a Northern Virginia mom with two children, works at Accenture, a global management consulting, technology services, and outsourcing company. Amy has a very flexible job setup—she has a job share with another employee, works part-time, and telecommutes from her home office. A nanny comes to her house to care for her children while she is working.

"I've been with Accenture for thirteen years since graduating from college and have worked in both consulting and in various roles within human resources/recruiting. I am now a senior manager in human resources.

I have two young girls, a three-year-old and an infant. I took five months of maternity leave with each of them, and I've just returned to work after having my second child. I have worked part-time since returning to work from my first maternity leave. Initially it was thirty hours (75 percent) in three days/week. I am now in a job-share arrangement where my partner and I each work a 60 percent part-time schedule; twenty-four hours in three days/week with one overlapping day to allow for transition between us. We have the flexibility to shift our workdays within the week whenever necessary to accommodate pediatrician appointments, school holidays, etc. It is so nice to know that on my non-workdays, there is still someone on point in my role to attend calls or address any urgent issues that may arise.

I have telecommuted since 2001—before my children were born. This is when I joined a global team, and as a result, I no longer worked directly with anyone in my local office. My boss and team were located in other cities, and we spend a lot of our time on conference calls anyway, so it made sense.

I have been telecommuting for so long that I take it for granted at this point, and I would be very reluctant to give it up if I were to change jobs in the future. You can't beat a commute that involves walking upstairs with your morning coffee while you are still in your pajamas! It does take discipline, however, to remain focused on your work vs. some household task you might be passing by. I also found that I missed the daily face-to-face interaction with people in the office, and as a result I do try to go into the office about one day a week.

Overall, I feel I have the best of both worlds with this arrangement. I am able to spend time with my children while also earning income and continuing my career, albeit on a slower track. However, as I don't view my career as my top priority anymore, this doesn't bother me. I'm confident that the fast track is waiting for me whenever I want to resume the pace!"

Working During School Hours

For many moms, working during school hours would be ideal, but is it possible? A growing number of companies allow employees to work very early hours, perhaps starting at 6 to 8 a.m., which may enable you to be home when your children's bus arrives. But there are trade offs; you will likely need to go to sleep very early, especially if you need to commute a significant distance to your workplace. You may be able to negotiate taking vacation time during your children's spring break (or put them in a day camp), but what about the summer?

Summertime Flex

Working flexible hours during the summer months may not be "the impossible dream" anymore at some companies. At GlaxoSmithKline, for example, staff can request working a reduced-hour schedule during the months of June, July, and August, if they want to spend more time at home while their children are out of school.

While some companies may not offer shorter summer hours, they may give you a more flexible schedule, especially if you are a proven employee. If you are a proven employee, you may want to negotiate working part-time and/or telecommuting during the summer months. For some moms, this may be the respite they need to care for their children while they're out of school.

Other childcare options include sending your children to summer camp during the summer months. Several companies, such as Abbott, set up on-site summer and school holiday camps for children of employees.

Long-Range Career Planning and Flexibility

As a career mom, your flexibility needs will likely change over the course of different phases of your professional lifetime. Lillian Zarelli Ryals, a director at MITRE Corporation's Center for Advanced Aviation System Development, for example, was able to work on a reduced-hours flexible schedule while her children were young, but now works full time. She presently flexes her time to arrive about one hour later every morning and is able to leave early once a week to meet with her child's academic coach. For the past three years, her husband has been a stay-at-home dad, enabling her to have a more flexible work-life balance.

In a Mom's Own Words
Lillian Zarreli Ryals, Executive and Mom

"After a three-month maternity leave, I worked full-time for the first year after my oldest child was born. At that point, I needed to spend more time with my son. I approached my management and requested a reduced schedule. My hope was to be able to spend each Friday at home with my son, as well as keeping any late evenings to a minimum. At the time, I was a mid-level manager and there was no precedent for this level of flexibility for mid-level managers in the company. However, my boss agreed to give it a try. Although I wasn't able to achieve a reduced thirty-two-hour workweek, my ability to handle certain activities from home on Friday and

(continued on p. 144)

(continued from p. 143)

in the evenings satisfied my need for increased time with my son. I repeated this pattern after the birth of my daughter. There were times when I worked from home, phoning into meetings, and other days when I brought my children to work with me for part of a day in order to be available for key meetings. My children were very comfortable at my office and enjoyed spending time there. My flexible schedule worked well for everyone. I continued to be promoted and assumed broader responsibilities over the next several years.

"My husband has been a stay-at-home dad for about three years. When he reached his thirty-year milestone with his company and was eligible to retire, we decided to make the change in order to improve our quality of life. We both found that the demands on our time as our children got older were creating too high a level of stress on the entire family. Previously, my husband and I had managed our work/home balance through combined flexibility of our jobs. Neither of us had previously stayed at home full time."

In a Mom's Own Words
Kerri Westburg, Mom and Flex-Working Professional

Kerri Westburg, a Northern Virginia mom with two sons, works on a flexible schedule for Booz Allen Hamilton.

"When I left the Air Force, I specifically looked for a company that had flexible work options so I could easily transfer offices when the Air Force transferred my husband. Booz Allen really fit that bill, and it has been that flexibility that has kept me with this firm. I've been with the firm for six and a half years and worked in Colorado Springs, CO, Norfolk, VA, and Arlington, VA. Continuing to have a flexible work arrangement has been a priority, and I have tried to choose clients that will support that even if the work itself is not my first choice. I've found my flexibility and adaptability to work with different clients in different work areas has really opened up my options in flex-work arrangements.

"I've telecommuted and taken advantage of flex-work arrangements at various times throughout my career with Booz Allen. I started telecommuting when my first child was three months old. My first daycare fell through and my backup daycare did not have room for another six weeks. I worked part-time from home until I was able to bring my child to daycare. I went back to work full time and only telecommuted on an as-needed basis until my child was six months.

"At that time, my husband deployed to Afghanistan and with no family in the area, I was in effect a single mom for five months. I telecommuted for two days a week, but still worked full time. This saved me up to two and a half hours on those days because I didn't have to take the time to dress in a suit and commute in traffic to work. It allowed me to run errands that can only be done M-F, 9–5, and take a sick child to the doctor's office (my child had ear infections three months straight, culminating in an ear tube day surgery during my husband's deployment). Telecommuting/flex schedule was really the only way I could've continued to work full time. This didn't just benefit me, it benefited my company and client as they did not have to lose a key team member.

"After my husband returned home, I telecommuted one day a week. When my child was fifteen months old I went to work part-time and telecommuted as needed for three months while resolving my child's health issues at the time. After, I went back to work full time, I telecommuted one day a week formally, and as needed, and have been doing so for the last two years. I've since had a second child as well."

Federal Government Offers Multiple Flex Opportunities

A comprehensive array of work/life programs and policies are offered to employees of the federal government in order to "create a more flexible, responsive work environment," according to the Office of Personnel Management (OPM) Work-Life Programs and Policy Office webpage: OPM.gov/Employment_and_Benefits/WorkLife/index.asp.

Federal workplace flexibility programs include alternative work schedules, leave programs, part-time and job-sharing programs, and telework opportunities. Many federal agencies provide childcare assistance by providing services including on-site childcare, resource and referral services, and a childcare subsidy program.

To access a ranked resource of the "Best Places to Work in the Federal Government," produced by the American University Institute for the Study of Public Policy Implementation, go to: BestPlacesToWork.org and click on "Work-Life Balance" and "Family-Friendly Culture and Benefits."

Advocacy Organizations that Promote Work-Life Balance

Many advocacy organizations have been established with the mission of researching and promoting work-life balance in the workplace. Here are just a few of the leading organizations:

- Catalyst, a nonprofit woman's business and professions research organization; Catalyst.org
- Center for Work-Life Policy, a work/life research organization; WorkLifePolicy.org
- Center for Work & Family, Boston College, a research organization focused on helping organizations create effective workplaces that support and develop healthy and productive employees; BC.edu/centers/cwf
- Families and Work Institute, a nonprofit research organization; FamiliesAndWork.org

- Sloan Work and Family Research Network, Boston College, online information and research about work and family; wfnetwork.bc.edu
- Workplace Flexibility 2010, Georgetown University Law Center, research and information about work/life policy and laws; law.georgetown.edu/workplace flexibility2010/ (click on "links" to access the sites for dozens of other work-life balance organizations).

Legislative Initiatives and How They Affect You

As a career mom, you may be interested in the legislative aspects of work-life policy and what our government is doing to help working moms and dads. To find out about the political and legislative aspects of work-life policy, access the site for the Sloan Work and Family Research Network, a nonpartisan organization, at: wfnetwork.bc.edu/policy.php.

On this site you can find out about the laws and statutes in your state and your rights related to flexible work. You can also research what bills are presently being considered by your state legislature. Armed with this information, you can contact your state representatives to show your support for family-friendly legislation that is of importance to you.

Issues that may be of interest to you include:

- After school care
- Dependent care
- Flexible work schedules
- Part-time work
- Shift work
- Telework and telecommuting

According to the Sloan Network, as of this writing more than three-quarters of the states in the United States have standing committees for workforce development, and one-third of the states have committees that focus specifically on families or children. Nearly every state has a business association or family advocacy group focused on some aspect of work-life issues.

In terms of overall workplace flexibility, twenty states have passed statutes that address the availability of flexible schedule options, twenty-six states have passed statutes concerning part-time work, and sixteen have statutes on the books about telecommuting, according to a Sloan report. To find out the statutes in your state, consult the website.

Summing It Up: Should You Go Back to Work?

For many moms, going back to work is not optional—for a variety of reasons you may need to get back to work and start earning an income. For others, going back to work will be a choice. Whatever your motivations, it's important to consider your own priorities in terms of work-life balance. Most moms—and dads—want and need a flexible schedule to care for their children and sometimes their own parents as well. Work-life balance is also important in terms of having time for your children, your spouse, and for yourself. A growing number of companies and organizations are recognizing the need and are instituting programs so that their employees have a more optimal work-life balance. It's beneficial for both the employees and for the companies in terms of productivity.

As a career mom, you should seek out employment opportunities that allow for an optimal work-life balance for you and your family. You can also try to make a difference by contacting your legislators to express support for "family friendly" laws and initiatives. The next time you go to the polls for an election—whether local, state, or national—be sure to take into consideration the candidate's views on workplace flexibility.

It is likely that companies will continue to expand their work-life benefits and policies in the short and long term. As the seventy-seven million Baby Boomers (those born 1948-1964) begin to retire, companies will do more to attract employees since there will be significantly more vacancies than employees in many industries. This will be advantageous to working parents because you'll be able to demand a more family-friendly workplace.

8 WHO AM I? A SECOND CHANCE TO DECIDE

"Success is having a flair for the thing that you are doing; knowing that is not enough, that you have got to have hard work and a sense of purpose."

—Margaret Thatcher, former Prime Minister of Great Britain, (born in 1925)

Being a stay-at-home career mom is an exciting time, both in terms of spending time with your children and being in control of your future career options. For some moms, their time at home gives them an opportunity to reassess their career goals and motivations. Back in high school or during or after college, most of us spent a lot of time on self-assessment and trying to decide who we were and what career to pursue. Many times it was stressful—yet exhilarating. Now, you can have a second chance to decide what you want to do and how to focus, or re-focus, your career.

Career changing is not a unique phenomenon in the nation's workplace. Most employees change their careers five to six times over the course of their professional life. Stay-at-home career moms are in an excellent position to change careers because they can use their time at home for self-assessment, overall soul searching, and preparation for a new career.

As a mom, your priorities may have changed. You may have chosen your first career for a number of reasons, including money, prestige, ease, family expectations, or just plain chance, and now you may want to look at different options. If you find that you are dreading going back to work in the career you left, or are just plain lukewarm about it, then you should consider new career options.

Self-Assessment: What Do You Want to Do?

If you're lucky, then you already have an idea of what you hope to do with your career when you return to work. Other moms may have some vague ideas, but are not sure how to pursue a career change toward that new job. Fortunately, there are numerous ways and resources to help you decide, including taking career assessment tests, consulting with a career coach or counselor, and self-assessment by journaling and mind mapping. You can explore new career possibilities via online research and by reading career books and publications, networking and informational interviewing, volunteering strategically, and more.

ASSESSMENT TESTS

As a first initial step, some career seekers take career assessment tests, including personality and type indicators, interest inventories, skills surveys, and values inventories. Two types of assessment tests are available: self-directed assessments, meaning that you can take and score the test without the assistance of a trained professional, and tests requiring interpretive assistance by a trained professional.

Assessment tests are controversial among some career practitioners because some test takers may be steered into unsuitable careers or away from appropriate careers, and because self-directed test takers may misinterpret the results without professional assistance. On the other hand, the results of these tests can give you new ideas for careers to explore, if you keep in mind that the results can in no way predict career success, or lack there of, in any career field. What they can do is give you a way to explore suitable options related to your interests and preferences.

But, none of these tests are a "crystal ball," so use your common sense when interpreting the results. If you find that you're consciously trying to influence the results, for example, if you are trying to ensure that the test points you to becoming a teacher, take heed. If this is the case, then you probably already know what you want for your next career and should start actively researching that career, regardless of your test results.

It's also advisable to take two or three tests and compare the results. If you see a trend, then this might point to a career that's worth investigating. On the other hand, if you get a result that doesn't appeal to you, by all means ignore it. While these tests have varying degrees of scientific veracity, in the end they're all subjective.

Free and fee-based career assessment tests and personality inventories are offered online via a number of sites. Some tests give immediate results for you to assess yourself. Others require assistance from an assessment expert.

For excellent round ups and comparisons of some of the on-line sites that offer assessment testing, consult: "Career Assessment Tools & Tests" via QuintCareers.com/career_assessment. html and the Riley Guide's Self Assessment Resources at Riley Guide.com/assess.html. To access tests designed by the Department of Labor (DOL), go to: ONETcenter.org/tools.html.

To find a qualified career professional to administer, score, and/or interpret your results, contact:

Your Local Career One-Stop Center

The U.S. Department of Labor sponsors a system of 2,000 career centers nationwide. Each center offers career counseling and job search services. To find out more, go to CareerOneStop.org and click on "People + Places to Help."

- U.S. Department of Labor Career One-Stop Center. To find the center in your local area, go to: ServiceLocator.org and enter your zip code to access your local center.
- Not-for-profit women's centers (use a search engine to find a women's center in your area).
- Community colleges. Most community colleges have career centers that are open to everyone who lives in their regional area, whether or not you have ever attended that institution.
- The college or university from which you graduated. Alumni career counseling services are available at most institutions.
- Career counselors and career coaches in private practice.

Should You Get a Career Coach?

These days, everyone seems to have a life coach, career coach, or career counselor to help them strategize. Coaching is a growing trend, especially for those at the mid to executive level. A career coach or life coach can help you with self-assessment, career changes, and overall strategy. Coaching can be done via the telephone, the Internet, or in person.

Generally speaking, a career counselor is a professional counselor with an educational background, likely a graduate degree, in counseling or psychology. Career coaches and life coaches typically may have a higher education, human resources, or corporate background, or other educational background, with additional training in coaching.

To find a career counselor or coach, consult people in your network for referrals. You should also check with your college alma mater's alumni office or career center. You can also find career coaches and counselors via online sites such as:

- International Coach Federation: CoachFederation.org
- National Career Development Association: NCDA.org

It's advisable to interview several coaches to find the best match for your needs and to find someone you like and trust.

Ask prospective counselors and coaches for references. Do your research and make sure you're enlisting the services of a competent expert. Rates for different types of coaches vary, with career counselors generally charging a higher per-hour rate than career coaches. In some cases, counselors and coaches may charge a fee for a set number of sessions rather than on an hourly basis.

Counseling and career coaching services at community colleges, universities, workforce development offices, and women's centers will likely be offered free of charge or on a sliding scale based on your family income, or offered at a comparably lower rate than services offered by private practitioners.

Self-Assessment

CREATIVE JOURNALING

If you are contemplating a career change, then you may want to consider starting a log or journal in which you can include creative thinking activities for investigating your career preferences and interests. The activities in your journal could be a mixture of analytical activities (lists, schedules, research summaries, traditional essays) and creative activities (random jottings, pictures, poems, mind maps—it's up to you!)

Here's an example of an activity that you could include in your journal:

Fill in the blank in the following sentence: "The career I have always secretly wanted was to be a/an _____."
Or, "Back when I was a child, my dream was to be a/an _____."

Don't censure yourself; your journal is for your eyes only. What did you write? Astronaut? Movie star? Chef? Animator? It could be anything. Realistically, the career choice that you come up with may not be your best choice. On the other hand, why not? Even if it's not realistic—for example, becoming an astronaut at age forty without the training or relevant education, your choice may be a clue to a new possible career. If you picked astronaut, then you could dissect that career choice and find out what appeals to you about it. Maybe it's the "adventure" aspect or perhaps the scientific component. Someone in this situation might end up in a career as a science teacher or writer, or you may want to consider working in a museum or planetarium. If you picked "movie star," then maybe you could consider acting in community theater, or teaching, public relations, sales, and so on.

Your journal is a place to use creative thinking to discover new career ideas to explore either on a self-assessment basis or with the assistance or input from a career coach. Here are some journal activities that might give you some new ideas for exploration:

- What new interests have you acquired as a stay-at-home career mom? How might those interests transfer into a career opportunity?
- List all of your friends and former colleagues who have had jobs that seem of interest to you. What interests you about these jobs?
- List famous or prominent people you admire. What do you admire about their careers?
- Where do you see yourself as a professional in ten years and then in twenty years? What is most important to you?
- List your top ten dream jobs, whether you are qualified for these jobs or not. What do you like about each job?
- What are your hobbies and interests? What are some jobs that might relate to these hobbies?
- What are you truly passionate about? Is there a career that might relate to that choice?
- Think about and list the aspects of past jobs that have bored you or made you watch the clock. What did you dislike about these jobs? Why?
- Think back to college. What courses did you love? What did you love about those courses?
- What courses did you dislike or make you watch the clock? What did you dislike about those subjects?

- What types of work activities cause you to lose track of time and fully immerse yourself in your work?

MIND MAPPING

Another way to explore your career preferences is via mind mapping. Mind mapping is a creative activity used widely in the educational realm by teachers. A mind map is a way to explore ideas and make connections. To make a mind map, you draw a bubble with a central idea in it that you want to explore and then connect that bubble to other bubbles with other ideas that occur to you as you think about the topic. Mind maps can be created by hand or on the computer using Microsoft Word, or other mind-mapping software. There are no rules—it is just an exercise in free thinking using a visual diagram. Some people find that mind maps enable them to visualize, connect, and explore ideas more clearly. You can create a mind map to explore ideas for new careers, business start-ups, prioritizing work-life balance preferences, and so on.

Researching Career Options

Once you have found some new career ideas, start your research process by accessing Internet resources and reading relevant career books. Your first stop should be the Occupational Outlook Handbook (OOH), which is published by the U.S. Bureau of Labor Statistics at BLS.gov/oco/. On this site, you can explore thousands of careers to find out the required training/education, an overview of job descriptions, earnings, and expected job prospects. To use this site, use the search function to enter the name of the job you would like to research or a general term for a field of study or job function, for example, "biology" or "writing." Multiple job possibilities will generally appear. When reading the material, be sure to note "related occupations" for other career ideas to consider.

Additional occupational information is available on the following government-sponsored sites:

- CareerOneStop.org
- CareerVoyages.gov
- O*Net online: online.ONETcenter.org

A number of privately owned sites provide comprehensive career information, including:

- CareerOverview.com
- QuintCareers.com
- Vault.com, click on "Occupational Profiles"
- WetFeet.com, click on "Career Profiles"

To find out still more about possible careers, Google job information sites that focus specifically on the type of job you are researching. To get an inside look at an industry, read and subscribe to some industry blogs and publications, which will give you a glimpse into the latest news, trends, and buzz in an industry.

Another research strategy is to find out more about successful professionals in careers that you are considering. Identify some of these professionals and check out their biographies online. Take note of key aspects of their career path.

Next Stop: Professional Associations

Professional associations and organizations are a virtual goldmine for information on careers. On many association websites, you will find comprehensive information on career preparation. To find relevant websites, consult the description of your intended career in the Occupational Outlook Handbook: BLS. gov/oco/. Professional associations are usually listed at the end of each career description. Other sources to find associations include:

- Weddles Association Directory, Weddles.com/associations /index.cfm
- JobHunt.org, click on "Associations and Societies"

Networking Strategies

Associations are also a great place to start your networking campaign to find out more about possible careers and to start making connections in that new career field. For more information on networking, review "Networking Is the Magic Key" in Chapter One.

As an initial first step, try to set up informational interviews with professionals in your chosen field. Ask people in your network for contacts or, if necessary, cold call or e-mail a prospective professional and ask them if you can meet with them for a brief informational interview to find out more about careers in that field. Emphasize that you're not asking for a job interview or even job leads—you're just gathering information.

When you meet with them, ask pertinent questions about what it is like to work in that field. Make sure you have done your homework before your meeting and are knowledgeable about that individual's company. Check out the environment, too. Will you feel comfortable working in this type of office or workplace? As a stay-at-home career mom, you should ask about flexibility and work-life balance trends in that field.

Job Shadowing

If you find that you've focused in on a particular career, why not request the opportunity to "shadow" a professional for a few hours or a day in their workplace? It may sound far fetched, but job shadowing is becoming an increasingly common practice as a way to learn more about a possible career. Job shadowing started as a way for young people—typically high school students—to learn about careers. Now, a growing number of professionals are letting adults shadow them at work.

You may be able to find people to shadow via your alumni or personal network. Job shadowing may not work in some industries, especially where security clearances are needed or confidential information is involved, but it is becoming increasingly acceptable in others. By job shadowing, you will have the opportunity to get an upfront view of a day in a particular career and see if it seems like a good fit for you.

Volunteering

Volunteering is another excellent way to find out about new careers without making a long-term commitment. If you're interested in animals, why not volunteer at the local animal shelter or veterinarian's office? Or, if you're considering a career change to nursing, check out volunteer opportunities at your local hospital.

Many stay-at-home career moms obtain new professional skills by volunteering, and then parlay those skills into a new career. By volunteering, you'll meet people and expand your network, enhance your resume, and find out if a new career choice might be a good fit.

For those who are considering a political career, be sure to start volunteering now. You might want to contact your local political party to find out about volunteer opportunities or help with a local official's political campaign. In the political industry, volunteering is an integral strategy to get the experience that can lead to a paid job.

Should You Consider an Internship?

Internships, or short-term work experience for college credit, are typically designed for undergraduate or graduate students. If you're in an academic program, be sure to consider internship and cooperative-education opportunities. In some cases, internships may be a requirement for a degree program or for professional certification.

Consulting, Contractual Work, and Freelancing

As a stay-at-home career mom, you may want to consider finding short-term consulting, contractual, or freelance opportunities in the career you've identified. This is yet another "try before you buy" setup. For example, if you're considering teaching, start subbing for a while. You'll quickly find out if it's the right environment for your personality and professional goals. For more information on seeking out these types of short-term job setups, see Chapter Six.

Coursework and Training

In some cases, you may need additional education or training to bridge to a new career. Consider taking an evening course at a local college or a weekend or one-day seminar, if necessary, to get up to speed and make new contacts. Review Chapter Two for information on short-term and vocational-training programs, certificate programs, and graduate education.

Is It Time for a Career Change?

After carefully researching possible careers by networking, volunteering, and perhaps taking on short-term contractual work, hopefully you will have a better idea if it's time to start the process toward a career change. Along the way, you may have sought out the advice and consultation of a career coach or counselor, completed assessment tests, and did a lot of self-assessment.

If you find out the answer is "yes!"—pat yourself on the back. Self-assessment is a lot of work, but it's essential to finding a career that will bring you professional and personal satisfaction. Career satisfaction is equally important for everyone, but as a mom re-entering the workforce, you may be in a unique position to have enough time to really think about and examine what you want to do next. You'll have less time later when you go back to work because you'll be both working and caring for your children. And as a stay-at-home career mom, you'll avoid the potentially awkward future situation of quitting a job to make a career change. Now is the optimal time to try to forge your path in the right direction. And let's face it, if you're going back to work mainly for your financial needs and have mixed feelings about it, your best scenario is to find a challenging and fulfilling job that you will love.

Re-inventing You

If you have decided that it's time for a career change, consider how you are going to re-invent yourself and create your new brand. It sounds intimidating . . . re-inventing *you* . . . doesn't it? To re-invent yourself, you are going to start over, to some degree. That said, you will likely find that you have many transferable skills that you used in your former industry—or at home as your children's caretaker—that can be used in the new career. For example, the skill sets involved with numerous job functions, including sales, public relations, management, writing, communications, public relations, etc., may transfer well from one industry to another. Or, the skills you have acquired from being at home, either via volunteering, or by caring for your children (teaching, for example), may propel you into a new career.

Keep in mind that some career changes really just mean making an industry change, not a career change—i.e., you can get a job with nearly the same functions and responsibilities in another industry. But if that is not the case, then you will need to learn and acquire new skills via volunteering, consulting/ contracting/freelancing, and self study. In some cases, you may need additional education and short-term training.

You may want to find a mentor in the new career field to help you with this process. To find a professional mentor, use your personal and professional network. You may be able to find someone who is willing to mentor you via the alumni office of the college you attended.

Creating Your Brand

Your career change strategy should focus on creating your new brand, the professional image you will carry into your job or industry. While it may be difficult to envision yourself as a "brand"—think about different brands of products. What makes that product unique? What is its main selling point? As a career seeker, you will want to create your own brand, in other words, the way that you are unique and what specialized skills you can offer employers. "Jack-at-all-trades"—people who choose not to specialize, tend to be less marketable because they have to approach the job market in a scattershot fashion. Instead, you should try to zero in on the types of careers that best suit your own particular skills.

To create your own unique brand, you will need to network assertively using both online networking sources and in person at professional associations and other organizations. You will need to identify, research, and acquire the skills and competency necessary for expertise in your new target industry. Then you can create a personal plan to create your new brand and find a way to make yourself stand out in terms of your expertise. Depending on your career goals, this may be a short-term or long-range process, but whatever the case, this will bring you closer to making a career change.

Is it worth the effort? Of course! Why should you reluctantly go back to a job that does not suit your professional or personal goals anymore? Making a career change will give you a second chance for personal and professional success and hopefully enable you to find a rewarding job that enables you to have an optimal level of work-life balance.

9 JOB FIELDS YOU MAY NOT HAVE CONSIDERED

"You must do the things you think you cannot do."

ELEANOR ROOSEVELT, FORMER FIRST LADY OF
THE UNITED STATES (1884–1962)

Prospective career changers have a myriad of possibilities for new careers. In this chapter, you will find some ideas for careers that are predicted by the U.S. Department of Labor, Bureau of Labor Statistics (BLS) to be the "fastest growing" by 2016. Also included is the general level of salary and the education or training needed to transition into these job options. And if you want to find out about the nation's "big money" careers, I include a list of the highest paying jobs in America, according to the BLS.

Speaking of money, if you want to segue to a new career that is open to career changers and also offers a potentially high salary, think: sales. Sales career options are discussed in this chapter.

Have you ever considered becoming a teacher? Many stay-at-home career moms think about teaching. As a mom, you may be volunteering at your children's school and have had a bird's eye view of the teaching profession. As a teacher, your hours will be the same as your children's and you will get the summer off. In this chapter, you will find out more about how and if you should consider teaching.

As a stay-at-home career mom "flexibility" is (or should be) your middle name. This chapter will focus on some of the high growth/high paying careers that may also have flexible hours.

So How Hot Is Hot?:
America's Top Growth Careers

Some career seekers may want to consider jobs that are listed among the "fastest growing" in America. If you're wondering about the accuracy of the BLS predictions, relax. Generally speaking, the BLS is right on the mark, and they update their ten-year projections every two years. That said, you should not choose a career solely on the basis of projected growth. On the other hand, if you find a career of interest then it may be worthwhile to see if your skills, qualifications, goals, and temperament might be a suitable match for it.

Education Pays

Rankings of the fastest growing careers include information on the required education or training needed for these occupations. According to the BLS, "education pays"—in terms of both salary and employability. Half of the thirty fastest growing occupations require a bachelor's degree or higher, and that number is projected to increase slightly by 2016.

For the purposes of this chapter, BLS growth rates for the occupations mentioned are ranked by the following criteria:

A+: 40 to 50 percent growth ("super stars" for projected growth)
A: 20 to 39 percent (amazing growth)
B: 11-19 percent (excellent growth)
C: 1-10 percent (still a very good "grade")

Since this chapter focuses on growth careers, jobs that are expected to stay at the same level or decline in growth are not included. Keep in mind that growth rates vary by region. To find out about occupation trends in your state, go to the website for America's Career One Stop: ACINET.org. If you want to find out about the projected growth rates for a career that is not included in this chapter, or more information about any of the included careers, go to the Occupational Outlook Handbook at BLS. gov/OCO/. For additional information about America's high growth careers, check out Career Voyages: CareerVoyages.gov. Be sure to check out the websites for relevant trade associations and organizations to find out more about the careers that may be of interest to you.

To find out more about continuing education, review Chapter Two.

In this chapter, median salary, as calculated by the BLS, will be identified as follows:

$$$$ = very high
$$$ = high
$$ = low
$ = very low

Specific ranges for these salaries are very broad. To find out the actual estimated median salary for an occupation, access the Occupational Outlook Handbook at BLS.gov/OCO/ and enter that job title into the search.

America's Top Twenty Fastest Growing Careers

1. Network systems and data communication analysts: A+, $$$$
2. Personal and home care aides: A+: $
3. Home health aides: A+: $
4. Computer software engineers, applications: A+, $$$$
5. Veterinary technologists and technicians: A+, $$
6. Personal financial advisors: A+, $$$$
7. Makeup artists, theatrical and performance: A+, $$$
8. Medical assistants: A, $$

9. Veterinarians: A, $$$$
10. Substance abuse and behavioral disorder counselors: A, $$$
11. Skin-care specialists: A, $$
12. Financial analysts: A, $$$$
13. Social and human service assistants: A, $$
14. Gaming surveillance officers and gaming investigators: A, $$
15. Physical therapist assistants: A, $$$
16. Pharmacy technicians: A, $$
17. Forensic science technicians: A, $$$
18. Dental hygienists: A, $$$$
19. Mental health counselors: A, $$$
20. Mental health and substance-abuse social workers: A, $$$

Show Me the Money! America's Top Twenty Highest-Paying Occupations

1. Anesthesiologists
2. Chief executives
3. Family and general practitioners
4. Internist, general
5. Obstetrician and gynecologists
6. Oral and maxillofacial surgeons
7. Orthodontists
8. Physicians and surgeons, all other
9. Prosthodontists
10. Psychiatrists
11. Surgeons
12. Airline pilots, copilots, flight engineers
13. Pediatricians, general
14. Dentists, general
15. Air traffic controllers
16. Podiatrists
17. Engineering managers
18. Lawyers
19. Judges
20. Computer and information systems managers

High-Paying Careers for the Rest of Us

You may look at this list, and sigh: "But, I'm not a doctor!" As you will have noted, thirteen of these twenty top-paying occupations are in the healthcare industry—including doctors, dentists, and psychiatrists. The average pay for an anesthesiologist, the number one highest-paying career, is $145,600+, according to the BLS; all of the top-twenty careers pay in the six figure realm. All of the top twenty require at least a BA, except air traffic controllers—the only career in the list of top-twenty highest-paying jobs that does not require a college degree.

But while you may not have an MD, other front-runners for income include various IT professionals, lawyers, marketing managers, and sales managers.

Front-Runners for Growth: Health-Related Careers

Leaving top-money projections aside, nearly three-quarters of job growth will come from three sectors: healthcare, computers, and education—including training and library occupations.

Careers in healthcare dominate the BLS's list of top-growth careers, and opportunities are expected to increase as America's seventy-seven million aging Baby Boomers increase demand for health-related services.

Healthcare services is the largest industry in the country, with more than fourteen million jobs. More than three million new jobs are expected to be created in the health-services sector by 2016—more than any other job sector.

If you have a strong interest in medical science and health, then you might want to consider a career change to this burgeoning industry sector. Aside from exhibiting tremendous growth, healthcare positions are generally both lucrative and flexible. Opportunities are widely available to work full time, part-time, or on a seasonal or contractual basis. Full-time workers may be able to work during specific shifts, for example, while their children are at school. Benefits may be available to part-time employees.

Growth jobs in healthcare require various training or education. For many types of healthcare positions, additional schooling/training can be completed in two years or less. While you may already have a degree in another subject, some of these health careers may be a good bet for a career change if you are willing to go back to school.

Fastest-Growing Occupations in the Health Sector

This list includes careers in pharmacy-related and dental industries, with information on required education, expected growth (indicated by grade), and projected salary (indicated by $).

Source: statistics excerpted from U.S. Department of Labor, Bureau of Labor Statistics, 2006-2016.

Professional Degree:
Pharmacists: A, $$$$
Chiropractors: A, $$$$
Physicians and surgeons: B, $$$$
Optometrists: B, $$$$

Master's Degree:
Physical therapists: A, $$$$
Physician assistants: A, $$$$

Bachelor's Degree:
Health Educators: A, $$$

Associate's Degree:
Physical therapist assistants: A, $$$
Dental hygienists: A, $$$$
Cardiovascular technologists and technicians: A, $$$
Radiation therapists: A, $$$$
Registered Nurses: A, $$$$
Respiratory therapists: A, $$$$
Medical equipment repairers: A, $$$
Diagnostic medical sonographers: B, $$$$
Medical records and health information technicians: B, $$
Nuclear medicine technologists: B, $$$$
Medical and clinical laboratory technicians: B, $$
Radiological technologists and technicians: B, $$$$

Post-Secondary Vocational Award:
Surgical technologists: A, $$$
Emergency medical technicians and paramedics: B, $$
Nursing aides, orderlies and attendants: B, $$
Dietetic technicians, B, $$
Medical transcriptionists: B, $$
Licensed practical and licensed vocational nurses: B, $$$

Moderate On-the-Job Training
Medical assistants: A, $$
Pharmacy technicians: A, $$
Dental assistants: A, $$

Short-Term On-the-Job Training
Personal and home-care aides: A+, $
Home health aides: A+, $
Physical therapist aides: A, $$

Spotlight: Is Nursing in Your Future?

Registered nurses make up the largest healthcare occupation—more than 2.5 million jobs. Job openings for nurses are expected to grow much faster than average—nearly by one-quarter. A nursing shortage presently exists throughout the country. For stay-at-home moms with the requisite skills and experience, this may be your incentive to go back to school to become a registered nurse.

There are three main ways to become a nurse. Complete:

- a bachelor of science in nursing
- an associate's degree in nursing from a community or junior college
- a diploma from an approved nursing program at a hospital

A master's degree is needed for some types of nursing careers, including nurse practitioner, nurse anesthetist, nurse midwife, and nurse supervisor. To find out more about nursing as a career as well as educational options, consult websites such as the American Association of Colleges of Nursing, AACN. nche.edu.

Growing Opportunities in Psychological and Social Services

This list includes information on required education, expected growth (indicated by grade), and projected salary (indicated by $).

Source: statistics excerpted from U.S. Department of Labor, Bureau of Labor Statistics, 2006-2016.

Master's Degree:
- Mental health counselors: A, $$$
- Mental health and substance abuse social workers: A, $$$
- Marriage and family therapists: A, $$$

Bachelor's Degree:
- Substance abuse and behavioral disorder counselors: A, $$$
- Social and community services managers: A, $$$$
- Medical and public health social workers: A, $$$
- Child, family, and school social workers: B, $$$

Associate's Degree:
- Occupational therapy assistants: A, $$$

Moderate On-the-Job Training:
- Social and human services assistants: A, $$

Computer Industry Leads the Way for Growth

While the 2001 dot-com bust may still not yet be "yesterday's news," opportunities abound and have been growing steadily in the computer industry. The number one and number two fastest growing careers in America are presently: network systems and data communications analysts—predicted to grow by 53 percent; and computer software engineers, applications—expected to increase by 45 percent. Other computer-related careers also rank highly on the list of fastest growing careers.

Many of the computer-related growth professions require at least a bachelor's degree. Some employers are seeking applicants with advanced degrees in computer science, computer engineering, or an MBA with a concentration in information systems.

But while a computer science degree is required for jobs such as database developer or software engineer, certificate programs are common for support and system administration positions, which are high-growth career fields. Certification programs for network and systems administrators are offered by a variety of vendors and product makers, such as Microsoft and Red Hat. Check with your local community college and local computer learning centers for other certificate opportunities.

According to the DOL, graduates of non-computer degree programs with additional coursework in computer programming, systems analysis, and information technology (IT) should be able to find jobs in the field.

Career changers may want to consider searching for an IT job in project management with a specialty in their past or present industry function, for example: healthcare or telecommunications. More than 90 percent of IT jobs are in non-computer industries, according to the Information Technology Association of America.

Flexible job opportunities are widely available throughout the computer industry, including part-time, telecommuting, and full-time/flexible positions. Computer professionals should be able to find plentiful consulting and contractual opportunities.

Fastest-Growing Computer Jobs
Listed by educational requirements, expected growth (indicated by grade), and projected salary (indicated by $).

Requiring a BA:
Note: salaries for all these positions estimated at $$$$.

- Network systems and data communications analysts: A+
- Computer software engineers, applications: A+

- Computer systems analysts: A
- Database administrators: A
- Computer software engineers, systems software: A
- Network and computer systems administrators: A

Requiring an Associate's Degree or Industry Training:
- Computer support specialists: B, $$$

Legal Field Offers Multiple Opportunities

Opportunities in the legal field continue to grow, especially for paralegals and legal assistants. Growth careers in this field include:

- Lawyers: B, professional degree, $$$$
- Paralegals and legal assistants: A, associate's degree, $$$$
- Legal secretaries: B, associate's degree, $$$

Education-Related Careers Makes Sense

Overall, education is predicted to be a fast-growing career field. Demand for preschool, kindergarten, elementary, and secondary teachers is expected to be "good to excellent," according to the BLS, depending upon the locality, grade level, and subject taught. Demand for teachers is expected to grow for all levels and sectors, except vocational education, which is anticipated to dip slightly. A continuing demand also exists for teacher's assistants. In the administration realm, a growing demand exists for administrators at the primary, secondary, and university level.

Be aware that the following growth statistics are for the nation as a whole. If you are interested in a teaching career, be sure to access the statistics for your state's growth and staffing expectations via your state's Department of Education website. It is also important to check with the offices for the district in which you hope to teach. You will find that projected needs vary significantly in different localities. An acute need for teachers exists in some areas, depending upon the grade level/subject.

Fastest-Growing Jobs in Education

Listed by educational requirements, expected growth (indicated by grade), and projected salary (indicated by $).

Requiring a BA or higher:

- Education administrators, preschool and childcare program: A, bachelor's or higher degree plus work experience, $$$.
- Postsecondary teachers: A, doctoral degree, $$$$
- Instructional coordinators: A, master's degree, $$$$
- Directors: religious activities and education: A, bachelor's degree, $$$
- Special education teachers: preschool, kindergarten, and elementary school, A, bachelor's degree, $$$
- Elementary school teachers, except special education: B, $$$
- Middle school teachers, except special and vocational education: B, bachelor's degree, $$$
- Secondary school teachers, except special and vocational education: C, bachelor's degree, $$$
- Special education teachers, secondary school: C, bachelor's degree, $$$

Education Jobs Not Requiring a College Degree:

- Preschool teachers, except special education: A, postsecondary vocational award, $$
- Self-enrichment education teachers: A, work experience in a related occupation, $$$
- Childcare workers: B, short-term on-the-job training, $
- Teacher's assistants: C, short-term on-the-job training, $

Have You Considered a Career Change to Teaching?

For some stay-at-home career moms, becoming a teacher would be akin to having it all. You will have virtually the same schedule as your children and get the summers off.

But, while it looks great from the outside, there are a number of factors to consider. First, you should not choose teaching solely for the hours. As a parent, we all agree that we need our teachers to be fully dedicated to the teaching profession, not just the flexible hours. Second, the hours may be a lot longer than it appears. You may not be able to leave at a certain time every day and may need to work overtime to get your work done. Most teachers work in the evenings at home preparing lesson plans, grading papers, and so on. You may have to go to meetings with administrators and other teachers after school. Secondary school teachers also may be required to run clubs and may be strongly encouraged to attend school sports or music events. And the summer . . . many teachers have to take course work and attend seminars to keep their license current. They also start preparing their lessons and curriculum planning for the next school year. Teachers often say that lesson planning and time commitments go down after the first year—if they end up teaching the same subjects at the same grade level the next year.

Are you still game? If you're interested in teaching, your first step could be to sign up as a substitute teacher. By subbing for a while, you will quickly find out if this is the right career for you. Teaching is intensely rewarding and a fulfilling profession for some people, yet overly stressful for others. It's important to find out where you stand before starting the coursework necessary to become a teacher.

Another route is to take a job as a teacher's assistant for an academic year. This will enable you to find out about teaching before making the big financial and time commitment necessary for the required coursework. One perk is that some school districts pay for their teacher's assistants to take teaching certification courses in the evenings. And while the salary may be comparably low, you will likely get benefits.

Paths to Licensure

A number of routes exist to becoming an elementary or secondary-level teacher, including the traditional route of obtaining a BA from a teacher education program. As a career switcher, you are more likely to obtain an MA from a teacher education program and then obtain a license, or obtain your license through an "alternative path to certification." Graduate-level and career-switcher programs are available via a number of colleges and universities in many regions. Coursework is sometimes offered in the evenings, on weekends, and / or during the daytime hours. Some programs offer "fast track" methods to completing your required coursework quickly; other programs will take one to two years. If you obtain your graduate degree, then you will be eligible for a higher starting salary when you start teaching.

Your first step for finding out about teaching programs is to consult the Department of Education's website: Ed.gov and click on "Teachers" and then "Find Teaching Opportunities" and then "Certification Requirements by State." This will link you to the homepage for your state's Department of Education.

On the Ed.gov homepage, you can also click on "Become a Teacher" and then "Training & Degree Programs." To find out about nontraditional licensure, click on "Center for Alternative Certification." Here you can search your state, region, and area of interest to find out about programs in your area.

ADMINISTRATION JOBS: PRIMARY/SECONDARY LEVEL

Opportunities are available in school district administration offices. Many of these positions are comparable to similar positions in the private sectors—i.e., human resources, secretarial, management, etc. You will likely be required to work during summer break.

If you're planning to become a teacher, consider whether you may want to aim for administration opportunities such as an assistant principal and principal down the line. Educational administration is a high-growth career field. Teachers will need to have several years of experience before starting coursework to qualify for administration positions.

ADMINISTRATION ON COLLEGE CAMPUSES

College campuses offer an array of professional and administrative positions. While these types of positions are generally year-round jobs, some colleges offer generous vacation and leave packages. At some campuses, employees receive tuition remission for themselves, their spouse, and their children.

Preschool Teaching May Be the Ticket

While the pay is typically low, some stay-at-home career moms may want to set their sights on becoming a preschool teacher at a private school or daycare. In many cases, no additional education is necessary. You may be able to start by volunteering in a preschool or daycare and take any training or coursework that is recommended by officials at that school. In some cases, you may be able to bring your child or children to work with you. If they are of preschool age, then you may receive free or reduced-price tuition.

Some stay-at-home career moms work at a preschool or daycare for a couple of years with the goal of becoming a director or manager. Others may want to start their own home-based preschool or daycare center. To find out more about home-based businesses, review Chapter Five.

Training is required to become a Montessori teacher. For more information, consult: Montessori.edu.

Have You Considered Sales?

If you're interested in a career change, but don't want to commit to further education, consider a sales career. To be successful in sales, you should be outgoing, enthusiastic, and possess "sales skills"—including tenacity and the ability to persuade. Sales careers are generally considered an "easy" career switch because these types of careers tend to be open to newbies. Once there, however, you have to prove yourself by selling a product successfully. If you cannot sell the product, then you will not last long in a sales career.

While there are many types of possible sales careers, here is a sampling of the sales careers that you may want to consider:

- Real estate: B, $$$
- Pharmaceutical and medical devices: B, $$$$
- Advertising sales representatives: A, $$$

- Financial—securities, commodities, and financial services sales agents: A, $$$$

Is Real Estate Flexible Enough?

For some moms, real estate is a natural choice. Real estate is a growth career field that offers significant flexibility. Training and licensure programs are short in duration—enabling a fast transition into this career. A college degree is optional.

On the downside, however, you will likely work while your children are at home—in the evenings and on weekends. This may work well if your spouse is at home with your children during those time periods. Some realtor moms like this setup because they can have time to volunteer at their child's school during the day.

Pharmaceutical Sales

Pharmaceutical sales is a high growth career field. Pharmaceutical sales reps do not need to have a medical or science background, but generally need to have a four-year degree in any subject. It's important to have an interest and aptitude for learning about medicine and science.

It is very competitive to find a pharmaceutical sales job, but the reward is a high degree of flexibility. In this job, you will spend your time on the road calling on doctor's offices, hospitals, and other medical facilities. It's a commission-only position, but your salary can be potentially very lucrative. You may be able to negotiate a part-time position and work while your children are in school.

Advertising Sales Representatives

Advertising sales is a high-growth and potentially high-salary career option. Big companies may prefer a college degree, while smaller companies may hire applicants with a high school diploma. Most training takes place on the job. Flexible job options are possible with this career, including the possibility of working part-time. Most advertising sales agents set their own schedule, but may need to work some evening and weekend hours.

Financial Services Sales

If you are financially savvy, then you may want to consider financial services sales. "Securities, commodities, and financial services sales agents" are an "A" ranked growth career with a very high median salary rate.

A college degree or MBA is required for many careers in the securities, commodities, and financial services industries. It's a highly competitive industry. But keep in mind that many positions will require a full-time and overtime commitment. Securities sales agents who work in call centers may be able to work on a shift basis.

Other Growth Fields in the Business/ Financial Sector

Several other high-growth business and financial careers may be of interest if you are seeking a lucrative career in business. These are listed by educational requirements, expected growth (indicated by grade), and projected salary (indicated by $).

- Personal financial advisors, A+, bachelor's degree, $$$$
- Management analysts; A, bachelor's or higher degree plus work experience, $$$$
- Market research analysts: A, bachelor's degree, $$$$
- Financial analysts: A, bachelor's degree, $$$$

Depending upon the workplace and specific job, these careers offer varying degrees of flexibility. Financial analysts and personal financial advisors typically work in offices or their own homes. Personal financial advisors meet with clients, generally in the evenings/weekends while they are not at work.

Management analysts and market research analysts may work for a firm or on a self-employed basis. As a home-business owner, they will have the flexibility to set their own hours in conjunction with their client's needs.

ACCOUNTING—THE LAND OF PLENTY FOR JOBS

Accounting is high-paying growth career with an excellent

potential for flexibility. Most accounting and auditing jobs in this field require a bachelor's degree. Many accountants choose to become certified as a Certified Public Accountant (CPA) to advance their careers. Strong growth in this field is projected because of stricter federal government accounting and auditing regulations. Some stay-at-home career moms work as accountants on a seasonal basis, often on a telecommuting basis.

A Few More Notable Growth Careers

While there are many careers with projected growth, here are just a few more of the potentially flexible careers that may appeal to you, along with required educational training.

- Multimedia artists and animators: A, bachelor's degree, $$$$
- Technical writers: A, bachelor's degree, $$$$
- Meeting and convention planners, A, bachelor's degree, $$$
- Interpreters and translators: A, long-term on-the-job training, $$$,
- Interior designers: B, associate's degree, $$$
- Fitness trainers and aerobics instructors, A, postsecondary vocational award, $$

Summing It Up

Flexible job opportunities may be possible with many of these career choices. As a stay-at-home career mom, your priority for your future career will likely be finding a flexible job that enables an ideal work-life balance. In this chapter, the focus was on high-growth and high-paying jobs, which may or may not be an ideal fit for your background, qualifications, interests, and overall career goals. Money matters to all of us, but you may or may not be willing to trade off a huge salary for a better work-life balance, if given that choice. It is never advisable to choose a job solely on projected growth or on the basis of its salary. No one should have to get up every day and go to a job that they dislike and that does not enhance their life. For all us, one of the keys to happiness is finding a fulfilling job that is a good match for their personal talents and ambitions.

But, that said, you may be able to fit it all together, depending on your skills, interests, and motivations. If you have a strong interest in one of the high-growth or high-paying careers, then you may be able to find suitable opportunities if you have the right background, qualifications, and are willing to take any additional training or education.

Growth expectations and projected salary may be a factor that you take into consideration for your longer term planning. For example, you may wish to get into sales with your eye on management later on. Or, you may want to make a career change to teaching with the eventual goal of becoming an administrator.

If your ideal career is not a "fast-growth" career, then keep in mind that there will always be opportunities in most careers for talented people with the right background and qualifications. It may be a little tougher to find a job, perhaps, but on the other hand, your enthusiasm and zeal for that particular job will shine through when you go to interviews because it will be the ideal job for *you*—potentially setting you apart from the competition.

In the next chapter, the focus is on how to find a full-time job. If you have been out of the workforce for a short while, then this may be an excellent refresher course. Long-term stay-at-home moms may be surprised about the changes in job search practices in the past decade.

10 ARE YOU READY? TRANSITIONING BACK TO THE WORKFORCE

"Have regular hours for work and play; make each day both useful and pleasant, and prove that you understand the worth of time by employing it well. Then youth will be delightful, old age will bring few regrets, and life will become a beautiful success."
—LOUISA MAY ALCOTT, AMERICAN AUTHOR, 1832–1888

Are you ready to transition back into the workforce? If so, now is the time to ignite the power of your personal and professional networks. Hopefully, you have maintained and expanded your network throughout your time at home. If not, don't worry—it's never too late to start networking. To review the fundamentals of networking, go to Chapter One.

Networking is the key to finding "unadvertised jobs"—which account perhaps for up to 85 percent of all job openings. Most jobs are unadvertised because employers prefer to hire people who they know and can trust or people who are referred to them via their own professional networks.

While you will find a myriad of advertised jobs online, remember that millions of other job seekers can also view these jobs. Competition for most professional jobs can be keen. One job seeker found out the reality of online competition when she applied for a job posting. Though she felt she was over-qualified for the job, she applied anyway. The company accidentally sent her an automated reply that included the e-mailed cover letters and resumes sent by hundreds of other job seekers who had applied for the same job; many, she said, were equally or much more qualified for the job.

It's still advisable to search for jobs via online sources, but savvy job seekers should focus primarily on networking. As a stay-at-home career mom, you may have been out of the workforce for a while and need to build your bridge toward the workforce via networking, which will prevent your resume from being just another of the countless "faceless resumes" in cyberspace.

Now is the time to tell all of the people in your network that you are seeking employment and ask for their assistance for job leads. You can also ask them for introductions to people they might know in your targeted industry. To review what you read in Chapter One, people in your network can include: friends, neighbors, and others with whom you interact in your community, including, but not limited to teachers, coaches, realtors, doctors, and so on. Your network will consist of former colleagues, people you have met while volunteering, people you met at industry events and other networking opportunities, etc. You never know who might know someone who can help you find a job.

Start with Former Colleagues

If you're interested in staying in the same career field, your first step should be to contact your former colleagues. Give your former colleagues a call, and ask them to meet you for coffee or lunch. They may know of opportunities in that company or others.

Focus on Online Networking

Be sure to focus also on online networking. These days some experts view it as almost "not professional" not to be on LinkedIn.com or another similar business networking site. On these types of sites, you build of network of online professional connections. If you are actively trying to build your network by volunteering, going to association meetings and networking events, etc., then you should have a few people to invite to start your network. You can also use the search to find former colleagues, former classmates, neighbors, etc., and invite them to join your network. With a few people in place, you can find out who your connections are connected to and ask for introductions, if desired.

You may be able to use LinkedIn.com or another business networking site to request informational interviews and find out industry and company information. Recruiters use these sites to search out suitable applicants, and jobs are also announced on these types of sites.

Informational Interviews Revisited

One key way to find out about unadvertised jobs is through informational interviewing. In your informational interview, you will ask the interviewer about opportunities in that career field and their advice on how to get a job. Remember that you are not asking for a job, just a few minutes of the interviewer's time. During the informational interview, ask for referrals to two to three professionals who they know in your target job field. Then, set up informational interviews with these professionals. Again, during the next round of informational interviews, ask for referrals to two to three additional industry professionals. Your networking via informational interviewing will expand outwards like a web. Be sure to thank each interviewer by sending an e-mail within twenty-four hours. Keep in touch with them occasionally by sending an e-mail updating them with your job search status. Tell them to please let you know if they know of a suitable job opening. If you make a good impression, then the people in your network will likely eventually tell you about unadvertised jobs.

The Hidden Job Market

Networking is the key to unearthing the "hidden job market"—

jobs that are not advertised. You can scope out unadvertised jobs via a variety of other sources, including:

- Professional associations: Association websites often have job boards and announcements for networking events. Many associations have online networking opportunities. Members are often given access to membership lists, which you can use to network with and contact employees at companies that are of interest to you.
- Alumni Associations: Check out the alumni website for the college(s) from which you graduated. You can typically search for alumni at specific companies and/or general industries that are of interest to you. You can contact these alumni to network and find out about opportunities at their company.
- Business press: If you read that an executive has had a promotion, for example, and you are interested in working at that company, write to the executive to find out if they will now need new staff. Or, for another example, if you read that a company has launched a new product line, contact them to see if they will need to hire more employees. This approach shows an excellent degree of initiative, which is likely to be impressive to a prospective employer.

Online Job Hunting

That said, you should keep your bases covered and also search out advertised job openings. If you find a suitable opening, then you can reach out into your personal and professional network to see if you know someone who works at a particular company. LinkedIn.com and other online networking sites can be useful here, too, because you can search out the name of a company and see if you know (or know someone who knows) a current or former employee of a company. You may be even lucky enough to find the profile and resume for a person who has the job or a comparable job to the one you are seeking. You can use this information to see how you stack up competitively. Similar information may be found by searching the alumni database for the colleges from which you graduated.

So . . . where to start? There are literally hundreds of online job boards. You are probably familiar with mega jobs sites such as CareerBuilder.com, Monster.com, and HotJobs.com. Take some time to peruse those boards and see what types of opportunities are available in your area. CraigsList.com is another big traffic website. For government jobs, check out USAjobs.com.

Smaller niche and industry specific sites may also be of use to you, for example, JournalismJobs.com or ITjobs.com. To search through a portal of job boards, go to Google.com/Top/Business/Employment/Job_Search/.

Be sure to check out both Indeed.com and SimplyHired.com. These sites pull content from many job sources, including the bigger boards, smaller niche boards, the *New York Times*, and Fortune 500 websites. You can save your search terms and have a customized e-mail sent to you daily with updates of newly posted jobs.

Many regional newspapers maintain an online presence, for example, WashingtonPost.com and NewYorkTimes.com. You can find a link to your local newspaper via NewsLink.org.

If you're interested in a certain company, go directly to their website. Career opportunities and application processes are posted on most company sites.

Sampling of Canadian Sites for Jobseekers

If you are in Canada, check out some of the following job sites:

- JobBoom.com
- Monster.ca
- Working.Canada.com
- Workopolis.com

Working with Recruiters

If you have been out of the workforce for a relatively short period of time, perhaps up to two years, consider working with a recruiter. If you have high-demand skills or qualifications, then they might work with you if you have an even bigger employment gap. But keep in mind that most recruiters tend to work with applicants with traditional work histories and might not accept a client with a resume gap.

There are two types of recruiters: *contingency recruiters* and *retained recruiters*. Contingency recruiters are paid only if they refer a person to a company who hires them for a job. Fees are paid by the company; the company pays either a flat fee or a percentage of the first year's salary. Contingency firms may send large numbers of resumes to a company where there is a vacancy.

Retained recruiters work on behalf of companies to find high-level executives to fill senior-level positions. They are paid whether or not the company hires the referred person, and the fees are paid by the company.

A headhunter, also sometimes called "executive recruiter," "placement specialist," or "search consultant" searches for candidates to recruit for a job at a specific company. They may search through their own database or search for candidates who are currently employed at other companies. Job searchers can send their resume to a recruiter for their database or apply for an advertised job that a recruiter is representing.

Keep in mind that it's advisable to work with firms that have their fees paid by the employer trying to fill the job. Job listings posted by recruiters can also be accessed via these sites.

To find links to executive search firms and headhunters, search "recruiter" and the name of your industry and location on any search engine. Or, find recruiters via resources such as:

- Quintessential Careers, Recruiter/Headhunter Resources, Directories & Associations: QuintCareers.com/recruiter_ directories.html, webpage with links to many online directories of recruiters.

- The Riley Guide's Job Banks & Recruiters: RileyGuide.com/multiple.html

Employment Agencies

Employment agencies assist job seekers with finding employment. To find links to federal and state-funded employment agencies in each state, go to Career One Stop: CareerOneStop.org and click on "State Job Banks" and the name of your state. State employment services are free to job seekers. Openings range from entry-level to six-figure professional jobs.

Private employment agencies are "for profit," and fees are paid either by the company or the applicant. If the fees are paid by the employer, the company works on its behalf to find the best-qualified applicants for that job opportunity.

When considering working with a privately owned employment agency, or recruiter or headhunter, be sure to verify that it is a legitimate operation. According to the Federal Trade Committee website, while many firms are legitimate, "others may misrepresent their services, promote outdated or fictitious job offerings, or charge high upfront fees for services that may not lead to a job." Check out any organization with the Better Business Bureau at BBB.org and get references before doing business with them.

Mom-centric Recruiters and Staffing Agencies

If you've been out of the workforce for a while and/or are looking for flexible work, you may want to check out some of the growing number of staffing agencies nationwide that help stay-at-home parents transition back into the workforce and/or find flexible employment.

Shannon Davis, CEO of BeyondMotherhood.com, a nationwide job board, said that many companies are seeking to hire stay-at-home moms who want to find flexible work. A few examples of highly flexible growth jobs for moms include textbook editing, corporate blogging, and marketing positions in start-ups hoping to sell products to moms.

But, according to Davis, "One of the biggest hurdles for stay-at-home moms is packaging themselves to be attractive to employers." Davis said that companies such as BeyondMotherhood.com help moms leverage their skill set to make them more attractive to employers by walking them through the process of creating a profile to best present their credentials and experience.

Kyra Cavanaugh, president of Life Meets Work, a Chicago-based nationwide flexible staffing firm agreed that companies across the country are becoming more amenable to hiring home-based professional employees. "There is a growing recognition on the part of employers that they need to look beyond the traditional talent pool," Cavanaugh said. "Returning moms bring experience, focus and commitment. Hiring them to work flexibly is the best way to attract them."

Maryann Perrin, a partner at Balancing Professionals, LLC, a flexible staffing agency in North Carolina added that her company was founded "to help change the way our community thinks about and does work. So much has changed over the last fifty years—including the demographics of the workplace; the structure of the American family; a rapid introduction of 'connecting' technologies, and a 24/7 global workplace—yet most companies use an Industrial Age model of work that focus on *time* and *place*." Balancing Professionals was set up to offer both advisory services to employers who want to facilitate flexible scheduling and to employees who want to work on a part-time basis.

Flexible staffing agencies can be a bridge to the workforce. Kathy Garino, a Roswell, Georgia, mother of three, for example, was a stay-at-home mother for more than four years and then successfully re-entered the workforce by finding her present job via Mom Corps, a national flexible staffing firm. She is now a part-time staff accountant with a mortgage company. According to Garino, Mom Corps made it possible for her to both re-enter the workforce and find a "family friendly" flexible position.

"I work part-time, twenty to twenty-five hours a week. I only have to go into the office for one half day per week. It's great!" Garino said.

Nationwide, there are a growing number of flexible staffing companies. Some are regionally based and others have a national focus. Some of the following specialize in helping moms transition back to the workforce, others in providing flexible work opportunities, and still others offer a combination of services.

To find additional flexible and career re-launch agencies, use Google to search terms such as "staffing," "part-time," "flex staffing," or "temporary placement" and your location and keywords for your career field.

SAMPLING OF MOM-CENTRIC FLEXIBLE JOB-STAFFING AGENCIES

- BalancingProfessionals.com, Raleigh-Durham, North Carolina, area. Focus includes flexible job-staffing services for job seekers.
- BeyondMotherhood.com, Ohio-based national board focused on helping moms find flexible jobs.
- ConnectMoms.com, Vancouver, Canada, area. Job board with flexible jobs suitable for working parents.
- EmployMoms.com, Hanover, NH, jobs nationwide. Focus is on placing moms in flexible professional jobs.
- FlexibleExecutives.com, Atlanta area. Job placement service that places seasoned executives in flexible corporate jobs.
- FlexibleResources.com, Connecticut, New York, and New Jersey offices. Flexible staffing and consulting firm for professional-level job seekers.
- Flexpaths.com: New Jersey-based global flex company assists both companies and flexible job seekers nationwide.
- Flexperience.com, San Francisco-based. Part-time, flex time, and project-based work in marketing, HR, finance, and law. Virtual opportunities anywhere.
- FlexworkConnection.com, Southern California region. Connects professionals with flexible work.
- Innovative-Outsourcing.com, Atlanta, GA, part-time staffing company that helps stay-at-home parents re-enter the workforce.

- JobsAndMoms.com, Connecticut-based, nationwide. Website for moms looking for flexible professional jobs.
- LifeMeetsWork.com, Chicago-based, nationwide. Flexible job information and job board.
- MomCorps.com, based in Atlanta, with offices in Charlotte, Chicago, New York, Raleigh, Washington, DC, and Boston. Connects moms with professional flexible jobs.
- Momentum Resources, Mom-entum.com, Richmond and Northern Virginia areas. Places professional moms in part-time jobs.
- My Part-time Pro: Secure.MyPartTimePro.com, PA-based, nationwide part-time professional job board.
- NeedlestackJobs.com, Ohio-based, nationwide. Flexible jobs for parents.
- On-Ramps.com, New York City-based flexible job consulting firm.
- Part-TimeProfessionals.com, places professionals in Orange County, CA. Nationwide job board.
- Smart-Moms.net, part-time employment in Raleigh-Durham-Cary, NC, and virtual opportunities anywhere.
- TenTilTwo.com, Colorado-based, nationwide. Part-time placement service.
- WomenForHire.com, New York-based, nationwide. Website includes job board, career expos, advice, and more.

In a Mom's Own Words

Beckye Young: Georgia Mom Who Returned to Accounting After Seven Years

Beckye Young, an Atlanta, GA, certified public accountant (CPA) was hired right out of college by the KPMG accounting firm in 1986. She worked in the accounting industry until the birth of her first child in 1993. She went back to work when she was pregnant with her second child, but then resigned when her child was born with special needs, which required her to stay home. During those years she had two more children.

"In the fall of 2003, when our youngest child was four, I decided to go back to work. I wanted to find a job that would permit me to work the hours our children were in school. As I had never had any problems finding a job since I became a CPA, and in fact had never looked for a job once hired out of college, I did not anticipate the trouble I would encounter. I had maintained my forty hours of required continued professional education to maintain my certification.

"I began calling recruiters and was told specifically that there were no positions for me. One recruiter even suggested I have more children! It was very discouraging to have recruiters tell you 'no,' as I know they want as many candidates as possible.

"In addition, I was sending out resumes to ads in the papers and professional newsletters that were asking for part-time workers. No one returned calls or responded favorably to my resume. It was very discouraging."

Young said she then found out about the Atlanta office of Mom Corps, a flexible staffing firm, through her personal network. She sent her resume into their office and received a reply the next day.

"As a part of the Mom Corps team, companies did not feel at risk taking on an employee who had not worked in accounting for nine years. As a part of Mom Corps, if it did not work out, they would simply replace me. However, I was never sent back by any of the companies that I worked for and was hired by one of them.

"It is wonderful to have someone believe I still had professional worth," Young added.

Re-Entry Programs at Corporations

A growing number of corporations have established re-entry in order to recruit highly educated and qualified professional moms back into the workforce. If you are an alumnus of a corporation, check their website and/or with their personnel office to find out if they have a re-entry program to bring back their employees. The Flexibility Alliance, a Washington state-based national organization, posts a list of companies with on-ramp programs on their site at FlexibilityAlliance.org/find flex.php.

You can also check out the following sites to see if your company is listed:

- Alumni.net
- CorporateAlumni.com
- Job-Hunt.org: click on "Company/Military Alumni Networks"
- LinkedIn.com, Corporate Groups

B-School Programs: Corporations Wooing MBA Moms

Several leading b-schools, including Harvard, Wharton, Dartmouth, and others—in some cases in conjunction with corporate partners—are taking steps to bring qualified stay-at-home moms back into the workforce by offering short-term executive education programs on their campuses. If you already have significant professional business experience, then you may be able to attend one of these transition-to-the-workforce programs.

Generally speaking, the curriculum's focus is getting up-to-date on recent business trends, finance, accounting, and technology. Career coaching, resume writing workshops, interview skills tutorials, and networking opportunities are typically offered.

SAMPLING OF UNIVERSITIES OFFERING CAREER TRANSITION PROGRAMS

To find out if there are additional programs in your area, contact your local colleges and universities.

Northeast region:

- Baruch College, Zicklin College of Business, New York City, "Opting Back in Program," three-day program: Zicklin. Baruch.Cuny.edu/, enter "Opting back in Program" into the search.
- Dartmouth University, Tuck Executive Education, "Back in Business Program," eleven-day residential program offered in New Hampshire and New York City on alternate weekends. Sponsored by Citi, in conjunction with Deloitte & Touche and American Express. For more information, go to Tuck.Dartmouth.edu, click on "Executive Education" and "Targeted Audiences." MBA or equivalent required.
- Harvard University, Boston, MA, Executive Education, "A New Path: Setting New Professional Directions," five-day residential program; "Charting Your Course: Discovering Working Options," two-day residential program for alumni. For information on both programs, go to Alumni. HBS.edu and click on "Career Development." Both programs are available to both alumni and non-alumni. While an MBA is not required, applicants need to have business experience.
- Massachusetts Institute of Technology (MIT), Cambridge, MA, "Mid Career Acceleration Program," ten-month part-time program, not restricted to alumni. web.MIT.edu/mitpep/map/.
- University of Pennsylvania, Wharton, Philadelphia, PA, "UBS Career Comeback: A Fellowship Program for Professional Women Re-entering the Workforce," highly selective program offered at no charge to participants. ExecutiveEducation.wharton.Upenn.edu, enter "Career Comeback" into the search.

Mid-Atlantic Region/Nationwide Seminar Locations

- University of Virginia, Darden School of Business, Charlottesville, VA. "Re-entering the Workforce" seminars, held at various locations nationwide. For more information, e-mail contact: Connie English at EnglishC@darden. Virginia.edu.

Midwest region:
- Xavier University, Williams College of Business, Cincinnati, Ohio, twelve-day program, "Back to Business Program," Xavier.edu/williams/, click on "Executive Education" and then "Back to Business." Twelve-day program. BA or MA required.

West Coast Region:
- Stanford University, Stanford, CA, "What's Next?" Career Transition Program, alumni.gsb.Stanford.edu/career events/career092407.html. Series of workshops on weekday evenings.

Re-Entry Programs for Legal Moms

Similar programs are starting to sprout up to lure lawyer moms back to the workplace, including:

- American University, Washington College of Law, Washington, DC, "Lawyer Re-entry Program," six-day program with follow-up, one-on-one career coaching sessions: WCL.American.edu/reentry
- Pace University Law School, White Plains, New York: "New Directions, Practical Skills for Returning to Law Practice," two-semester, three-part bridge program, for lawyers who hope to re-enter the career field. Pace.edu/page.cfm?doc_id=27383
- University of California Hastings College of Law, San Francisco, CA. Program of courses for returning lawyers. "Opting Back in Program": PARDC.org/Optin/—virtual program available to attorneys located anywhere in North America.

Navigating a Job Fair

Transitioning stay-at-home career moms should consider attending job fairs. Job fairs and expos can be excellent venues for meeting employers and finding out about job opportunities. Women for Hire, a New York-based national organization, runs job expos for professional women at locations in many U.S. cities. To find out more, go to: WomenForHire.com.

Tory Johnson, CEO of Women for Hire and workplace contributor for ABC's *Good Morning America*, said, "Attending a career expo is one of the best places to network. You can 'window shop'—go booth to booth gathering information about who's hiring and what's out there, which is especially valuable if you're just starting out. Or you can attend with a very specific focus: You're there to sell yourself to a particular employer."

Navigating a job fair can be tricky—it will likely be very crowded and many job seekers will be competing for the attention of the interviewers. Johnson emphasized that you need to project confidence at a job fair. "The best way to project confidence is to feel like you're worth it and that you have something to offer. That means smiling, standing tall, maintaining eye contact, and being articulate. Sounds simple, but it works. Speaking oh-so-softly, averting your eyes, shoulders slumped and not projecting an enthusiasm for yourself is a confidence killer. An employer must know you believe in yourself before they are willing to believe in you."

Johnson advises moms to network with other job seekers at career expos, who may have "advice, leads, or something to help you with your search."

"You won't benefit from that if you aren't willing to put yourself out there," commented Johnson. "Introduce yourself to strangers. Sometimes nothing comes of it; but other times something great happens."

More tips for success at job fairs and expos:

- Dress professionally.
- Bring a well-crafted resume.
- Consult the job fair's website to find out which employers are planning to attend. Do your homework—find out about the company and interviewer, if possible.
- Come prepared with your "thirty-second commercial"—

your brief introduction to who you are and what type of opportunity that you hope to find.

- Be prepared for a "mini interview."
- Arrive armed with questions that you can ask the employer.

Be sure to ask for a business card or write down the names of the interviewers that you meet. Follow up within twenty-four hours with an e-mail thanking them for taking the time to talk to you. Send your resume, if requested, or ask if you can send it to them.

Other sources for finding job fairs in your area include:

- Career Builder career fairs: CareerBuilder.com/jobseeker/careerfairs/
- Employment Guide: EmploymentGuide.com, click on "job fairs"
- Monster Job Fairs: Resources.Monster.com/job-fairs/

Volunteering as a Job-Search Strategy

Another strategy is to volunteer strategically, that is, find a volunteer position in a company where you may want to work. For example, if you're interested in working for a nonprofit organization, volunteer to take a part-time position there and make yourself "indispensable." When a suitable opportunity opens up, you will likely be the first person they consider. While volunteering, you may also find out about opportunities in other affiliated organizations. You will also be able to expand your network and likely be able to get an up-to-date personal recommendation. As a stay-at-home mom, you may have already volunteered for a number of organizations and may be able to parlay those experiences into a professional job.

In a Mom's Own Words
Blair Wilson, Twenty-Year Stay-at-Home Mom Turned Mayor and Executive

Blair Wilson, a New Jersey mom with four grown children, was a stay-at-home mom for twenty years and was then elected mayor of Mountain Lakes, NJ. She presently serves as a town councilperson and is the executive director of Morris Habitat for Humanity, a large nonprofit organization with eleven employees and 2,000 volunteers.

Wilson got married several months out of high school and promptly started a family. When her children were young, she went back to college, first taking one or two courses and then eventually increasing to a full-time schedule. She graduated twenty years later. Her husband was busy climbing the corporate ladder so she shouldered most of the responsibility for raising her children.

Wilson said that volunteering enabled her to make the jump from staying home to becoming mayor. "I think I'm the type of person who needs to always be busy, and I thought that as a stay-at-home mom, my role was to get involved in my kids' activities—cub scouts, girl scouts, PTA, etc. So I would go and volunteer wherever I was needed," Wilson said. At the same time, she was also actively involved in her community—in the League of Women Voters, the Woman's Club newcomer's club, and the Junior League.

"I always said that I would help out—from writing a weekly column in the newspaper to a monthly column in a local newsletter, from being a worker bee on committees to eventually holding leadership positions in whatever organization I was in. In fact, I became so involved that at some point my husband said that I should be earning money for all the work I was doing. But I liked the flexibility, and I was learning all the time . . . learning the computer, learning how to write, learning budgets, learning how to be organized, how to get along with people who don't have to be doing

(continued on p. 198)

(continued from p. 197)

what they're doing, learning how to negotiate, how to ask for money, for services, how to run events, how to study issues, to gain the confidence that one's opinion counts, that one's voice can be heard, etc.—all perfect training issues for politics and then eventually working for a nonprofit," Wilson said.

"I was president of the League of Women Voters when all the above training proved to be almost more valuable than my college courses. It was hands-on training, real-life stuff. Being a stay-at-home mom gave me the flexibility to learn a lot about real life as well as allowed me to be around for my children," she added.

Wilson was asked to run for town council while she was president of the League of Women Voters. Soon after she was elected, she found a job working as a housing counselor and program director for a home-ownership center. During the five years that she worked there, she was elected to two four-year terms on the town council, two years as a deputy mayor and one year as mayor.

"The opportunity to apply for the executive director of Morris Habitat opened up, and although I had just divorced, sold my home of twenty years, downsized into a smaller home, and had my last child go to college, I took the job when it was offered," Wilson explained.

Wilson advises stay-at-home moms to keep their skills current by volunteering. "The best thing is to not just stay at home, to get involved in the community. Some people like me can't say 'no' so we get ourselves over-involved, but women don't have to be like that; they should start by getting involved in their kids' school, their church, their municipality, or even the local hospital or nonprofit. Volunteering is a way to hone your skills, develop new ones or just keep current with what you already know," Wilson said.

Nonprofit Jobs May Be Open to Career Moms

If you're interested in a career where you can make a difference, consider working at a nonprofit organization—whether you start as a volunteer or as a paid employee.

Here are a few websites for finding nonprofit job leads:

- Deep Sweep, nonprofit job listings for executives, Deep Sweep.com
- Nonprofit Career Network: NonprofitCareer.com
- Opportunity Knocks, OpportunityKnocks.org
- Philanthropy Careers: Philanthropy.com/jobs
- Work in Nonprofits/Canada: WorkInNonprofits.ca

In a Mom's Own Words

Lisa Akers, Rocket Scientist Who Stayed Home for Five Years

Lisa Akers, a Denver, Colorado, mom of two children stepped out of a position as a satellite systems rocket engineer to stay home with her two children. During this time, she launched "Be Still and Knit," a home-based knitting company: BeStillAndKnit.com, which she continues to operate on a part-time basis.

"I was a satellite systems design engineer before taking five years off to be a mom to my two children. Just this past month, I've gone back to work full time. During my time off, I was running my own business, and still am, but have now started working for a contractor on the NASA Orion program to replace the space shuttle. I had planned to wait a few more years before returning to work, until my children were both in school, but I was called by a former co-worker and offered a higher-level position than I had imagined possible after being out of the workforce for so long. Those opportunities don't often come along, and I couldn't turn it down. It's been a challenge working with young children—and paying for childcare, but it is very rewarding to me to be back launching rockets!"

(continued on p. 200)

(continued from p. 199)

While Akers said she was not able to keep up with techno-
logical developments in her industry while she stayed home
because of the nature of that industry, "I did my best to keep
up with the latest news and keep in contact with people in
the industry. Overall, keeping in touch was more important
than keeping up. By remaining known in the community, I
was in a better position to be called on when the perfect job
came open. Plus, I was well-regarded in the industry, so my
reputation has been very helpful in my getting called back.
There has been a lot of learning to do with my return to work,
but fortunately, I am able to do much of that on the job."

Job Hunting Clubs

If you're looking for moral support and camaraderie, consider
starting or joining an existing job-hunting club or support
group. The group can work together as a team to help each other
with networking, job searches, resumes, etc. Each of you will
be the "eyes and ears" for one another. To locate a job-hunting
club, check with your state's employment office. To find an
existing job club in your area, go to: JobHunt.org and click on
"Job Clubs, Networking and Job Search Support by State." You
can join or start your own group via MeetUp.com. If you are
over forty years old, check out "40 Plus," a job club located in
various cities nationwide. Use a search engine to find your local
branch—each location has a separate website.

But What If You Need a Job "Yesterday"

If you're in a situation where you need to start earning money
right away, perhaps because of a divorce or if your spouse
becomes unemployed, consider temping. Temping is a great
way to earn cash, build your connections, and reestablish
yourself in the work world quickly. While temping, be sure to
continue your active job search on your nonworking hours. If
possible, you may want to take a day off each week to focus
exclusively on your long-term job search.

In a Mom's Own Words
Beth Mansfield, Transitioned Back after Five Years at Home

Beth Mansfield, of Ventura, California, transitioned out of the workforce to be a stay-at-home mom after her daughter was born. Five years later, she jumped back to the corporate workforce. "I went from planning play dates for my daughter to flying on a corporate jet with the CEO in a couple of months," Mansfield said. Mansfield is the public relations manager for CKE Restaurants, parent company of Carl's Jr. and Hardee's hamburger chains.

"A friend who I had worked with at a different employer was now with my new company and recommended me for the job. The position had been open twice before a couple of years ago, and I declined to interview because I wasn't ready to go back to work.

"When I interviewed last summer, I was very prepared, having done quite a bit of research on the fast-food industry. I was very confident in my abilities and was ready to be a professional again. I ended the interview with the vice president by saying, "I'm ready to get back in the game!" The woman I replaced only had a couple years of experience so they were able to hire me, a professional with twelve years of experience, for less than market value. I was willing to take less money in order to prove myself since I had been out of the profession for five years. My five-year absence from the profession wasn't really an issue because of my years of experience."

As a temp, your initial pay may be comparably low, but temping may lead to a permanent job. According to the American Staffing Association, twelve million employees nationwide were hired initially as temps. Temps are not limited to secretarial positions; opportunities are available in job functions as diverse as accounting, editing, paralegal work, and more. For more information, review Chapter Six.

Shannon Davis, CEO of BeyondMotherhood.com, advises moms who need a job immediately to register with online job boards and set up a search agent to be notified when a job is listed that matches their desired profile. It is also helpful to be proactive by posting resumes online on job boards, according to Davis.

Summing It Up—Job Hunting

Let's face it—job searching is a tedious practice, and most people will need to search for jobs a number of times during their professional lifetime. As a stay-at-home career mom, you may now have to face the hurdle of getting a professional job after a hiatus at home. But you can do it. Not only is the nation's workplace becoming more flexible and amenable to parents re-entering the workplace, but the Internet has enabled job searchers to find out about a literal world of opportunities. The next step is to craft an excellent resume. But how are you going to explain your resume gap of two, ten, or twenty years at home? Find out in Chapter Eleven.

11 PAPERWORK 101 FOR PART-TIME AND FULL-TIME JOBS

"Just don't give up trying to do what you really want to do. Where there is love and inspiration, I don't think you can go wrong."
—ELLA FITZGERALD, AMERICAN VOCALIST, (1917–1996)

Resumes are integral to your job-hunting success. This chapter focuses on how to create a resume that highlights your volunteer and other professional successes as a stay-at-home career mom. Job seekers need to create a professional resume that is targeted carefully for specific jobs.

This chapter focuses on the specifics of creating a resume for re-entering the workforce. General information on creating resumes is available in numerous books and on hundreds of websites. If you're not familiar with general resume writing, check out a few books and websites. Here are a few examples:

- QuintCareers.com, click on "Resumes"
- RileyGuide.com, click on "Resumes & Cover Letters"
- Vault.com, click on "Job Advice" and "Cover Letters"
- WetFeet.com, click on "Resumes & Cover Letters"

Resumes 101

If you have been out of the workforce for a number of years, keep in mind that you will need to create both a regular and an Internet version of your resume. When you are applying for jobs, check the company's website for instructions on the type of resume that they require and how it should be submitted. Many companies will not accept unsolicited attachments because of concerns about computer viruses. You can telephone or e-mail the company's human resources office to find out their application requirements. If you are not able to get in touch with someone, paste your resume into the body of the text of the resume.

Internet Resumes

While most companies accept regular resumes, you may be required to create a plain text resume. Plain text resumes can be scanned without creating formatting issues, because they do not have the "bells & whistles" you have in your regular resume: bullets, fancy fonts, italics, bolding, underlining, etc. In the past, many companies required this type of formatting, but many are now moving away from this requirement. If you need to create a plain text resume, consult some of the resume-writing and job-search websites.

Basic Rules for Creating Resumes

Basic rules for creating effective resumes include:

* Keep it short (one to two pages, maximum)
* Keep your language succinct
* Proofread scrupulously—make it error free
* Use "action words" to describe your accomplishments: for a comprehensive list of resume action words, check out this list from the Harvard University, Office of Career Services: OCS.fas.Harvard.edu/students/resources/resume_actionwords.htm

But How Do You Bridge Your Job Gap?

As a stay-at-home career mom, your resume will need to reflect your accomplishments and the skills you used during your time at home. When creating your resume, be sure to highlight two critical factors. Describe *exactly* how you are up-to-date with:

- technology
- your career field

To show your competence in technology, include your computer skills (Word, PowerPoint, Excel, etc., and any programs specific to your job objective and industry) on your resume. Take a computer class in your community, if needed, and list it.

In terms of your career field, be sure to include any continuing education courses you have taken and/or additional degrees. List the names of your affiliations with professional associations. Include any recent articles you have written, speeches you have given, or any other examples of how you have kept up with your career field. In other words "show, don't tell." Do not just write "I am up-to-date with the X industry"—highlight on your resume precisely how you have maintained and/or updated your skills and knowledge base.

Categorizing Your Work Experiences

If you worked part-time, telecommuted, consulted, etc., then you don't have a gap in your resume. Part-time employment should be listed on your resume in the same way as a full-time job. You can list "part-time" or "reduced hours" in your description of the job on your resume.

Consulting and contractual jobs, including temping, should also be listed as a job. If you temped for numerous companies, just list the companies that you worked for most often, those where you gained the key skills you are seeking to use, and/or the agency with whom you were contracted.

If you were self-employed or ran a home-based business, list it as a job as well, and describe all of the skills that you used to run this business. Employers will be impressed by the initiative and repertoire of skills you gained as a business owner.

Home-schooling parents should detail their teaching responsibilities in their resume as a job in the same manner as any other type of home business.

Volunteering Experiences Integral

If you have a resume gap from being at home, then your best course of action is to fill it in with your volunteer experiences. Your volunteering experiences will be an integral component of bridging your resume gap.

But what if you did not volunteer or maintain your skills? In your case, take the following approach: find and start one or two volunteer opportunities right away. You may want to take on a short-term volunteer project on a virtual basis. To find virtual volunteering opportunities, access USAfreedomcorps. gov. Or, volunteer in your children's school. To best enhance your resume, try to find volunteer experiences that are relevant to your career goals.

On the other hand, all moms, whether you have had volunteer experience or not, may want to include "mom skills" on their resume, if applicable in some way to the job they are seeking. For example, if you're interested in teaching, daycare, nursing, or other children-related or caring professions, be sure to highlight your skills as a parent. Such skills include caring for children (and your elderly parents, if applicable), organizing their activities, supervising homework, planning menus, and cooking, etc

Other household skills that may or may not be relevant to the job you are seeking include general household management, accounting (your bills), logistics (car pool), etc., and the amorphous "organizational skills." Should you include these skills? Probably not. These types of skills will be implied when you list "Stay-at-Home Mom" on your resume. If you are fortunate enough have an interviewer who is a parent or understands what parenting is all about, then they will understand the tremendous amount of work and responsibility that stay-at-home parenting involves.

But, if your job objective can somehow relate to the skills you gained at home, carefully consider whether you should include it on your resume. For example, "organizational skills" at home might translate well on a resume for a job for a personal scheduler. Or, for instance, you might consider adding your financial responsibilities at home if you are actively managing your retirement and stock portfolio and are vying for a job in a bank. On the other hand, whether we like it or not, some hiring managers will view these experiences with skepticism. As a stay-at-home mom, you did not have a supervisor, performance appraisal, salary, etc.—so some prospective employers may find it difficult to quantify the quality of your experiences. And some hiring managers are still "old school" in their thinking and don't understand that at-home experiences can and do transfer into the workplace.

For many stay-at-home career moms, the central focus of your time at home on your resume will be your volunteer work history. It's not necessary to identify such positions as "unpaid" on your resume; the emphasis on your resume will be on identifying the skills you acquired in these volunteer positions. Remember that while you were serving as a volunteer, other people were doing the exact same activities and using the same or comparable skills for pay in an actual job.

When listing your volunteer positions, emphasize positions that included job functions directly relevant to your targeted job. For example, if you were the head of fundraising for a soccer league and are applying for a job as a professional fundraiser, be sure to highlight those volunteer responsibilities on your resume. As another example, if you were a Girl Scout cookie sales manager and are now vying for a sales job, focus on that experience in your resume.

Some volunteer positions may have less obvious ties to jobs for which you are applying. Take some time to write down everything you did in each volunteer position and dissect the actual responsibilities that you had and skills that you used in that position. Consider how these skills might help your candidacy for the type of job you are seeking and add it to your resume.

You may find that some volunteer positions don't have ties to your future career. Depending on your job objective, these jobs may include: room mom, field trip chaperone, etc. These jobs can be described together in one section of your resume with wording such as: "Active school, community, and church volunteer. Helped out with various activities and functions."

A few words of caution—don't include volunteer positions that you only did for a very brief period of time. If you volunteered in your child's classroom one hour or one day, that's great, but don't include it. Would you put down a job you did for one hour or one day? But if you organized a one-day event over a period of time, then go ahead and include it. Also, don't exaggerate your experiences or the competencies that you gained in any volunteer job. Not only is it ethically wrong, but interviewers may ask for references and check out your background.

What Type of Resume Do You Need?

There are three types of resumes: chronological, functional, and combination. Chronological resumes are the traditional resumes where your experience is detailed in reverse chronological order. This is the best option for job seekers who have maintained a consistent full-time job history. If you have worked part-time, consulted, ran a business, etc., then this may be a good format for you. If you are bridging your gap with volunteer experiences, on the other hand, it is probably best to consider a functional or combination-style resume.

In a functional resume, the job seeker lists relevant experiences under specific skill-cluster headings. For example, a prospective sales manager might list relevant experience, including as a volunteer, under the following categories:

- Management Skills
- Marketing Skills
- Sales Experience

Functional resumes are an excellent choice for women who have been out of the workforce for a period of time and/or for career changers. In this resume format, you emphasize your skills rather than the consistency in your job history. You may not need to mention the gap in your work history if you have enough relevant experience.

That said, many employers prefer to see a combination resume, which is a hybrid of the chronological and functional resumes, because it is less difficult to discern your actual chronological job history.

In a combination resume, you will list your skills in clusters at the top of the resume—including as a volunteer—and then include a reverse chronological job history at the bottom of the resume. This resume can be an excellent format for most stay-at-home career moms because you will be able to target your skills to particular types of job opportunities.

In the chronological job history section of your resume, include "Stay-at-Home Mom," the dates, and a summary of your key volunteer and recent educational accomplishments, which you will have already described above in the skills summary section of your resume. After that, include the jobs you had before staying home in reverse chronological order.

Here are two examples:

- Stay-at-Home Mom: 2000-2008, Summary: During this time, I served as a neighborhood swim-team vice president for two years and was an active volunteer in the neighborhood schools. I managed a major campaign for my church to bring supplies to Hurricane Katrina victims.
- Stay-at-Home Mom: 2004-2008, Summary: During this time, I was PTO vice president (2004-05) and an active volunteer in the elementary school. I completed a paralegal certification program in 2008.

Some experts advise you to "de-emphasize" the parenting aspect of your time at home because future employers may fear that you will not make their workplace a priority. While this may be a concern, stay-at-home career moms are advised to seek employment with "family friendly" companies that value work-life balance. Would you really want to work for a company where you need to hide your status as a parent? On the other hand, there is no need to put the number or ages of your children on your resume. As long as you have your childcare arrangements in place, these details are not relevant to your status as a viable job candidate.

Should You Take the Dates off Your Resume?

It's well known that subtle and obvious age discrimination exists in the workplace. Some experts advise job seekers to leave the dates off your resume if you graduated from college or graduate school more than fifteen years ago and/or only include jobs that you had in the past fifteen years. Obviously, employers will find out how old you are when you complete their formal application and/or they do a background check. It's not that you want to "hide" your age, but avoid discrimination in the first round of your resume being circulated in a company. In some ways, it is a moot point, anyone can use the Internet to check a person's age on certain websites in seconds, but, chances are that they will not be that curious.

A factor to consider: do you want to work for a company that would discriminate against you because of your age? Some experts argue that you don't want to present yourself as overqualified for a job if you have extensive job experience, but, if at all possible, wouldn't you prefer to compete for jobs at your actual level of experience? Also, remember that not everyone hiring you will be your junior in terms of age. Many hiring managers will be in their thirties, forties, fifties and older and will value both your professional qualifications and your "life experience" in terms of maturity.

Whether you leave the dates off is a judgment call that you will need to make. Some stay-at-home career moms choose to leave the dates off their college graduation. But, as a stay-at-home career mom, it is generally advisable to include all of your relevant professional jobs and the dates, even if you worked there more than fifteen years ago. If you have been out of the workforce for a number of years, then you may need this experience to get a job, and it may be relevant to your current career objectives. You will need to put the dates, in terms of the years (i.e., 1998-2002), but can delete the actual months.

However, depending on your career objectives and number of years out of college, you may now want to consider de-emphasizing your college internships and summer jobs on your resume. Instead of including a detailed description of your college internships and summer jobs, mention your internship briefly in the "Education" section of your resume, for example:

BA, University of Maryland
Major: International Relations
Academic Internship: researcher, World Bank (one year)

Should you delete jobs that are clearly not relevant to your job objectives? Probably not, but you may want to "de-emphasize" such job experiences on your resume, while at the same time, if possible—identifying any relevant transferable skills. That said, be sure to keep your resume to one to two pages, with one page being the preferable option. If you need to abbreviate your experiences, de-emphasize those jobs that were least relevant to your current job objective. But if you have pages of experience, then you may need to consider editing out some of your earlier entry-level jobs.

If you need help with resume writing, consider hiring a professional resume writer. Links for finding professional resume writers include:

- National Resume Writer's Association: NRWAweb.com
- Professional Association of Resume Writers & Career Coaches: PARW.com

Free or low-priced resume assistance can be found via:

- CareerOneStop.org: click on your state to find workforce centers in your area.

- Career Centers in the college(s) from which you graduated.
- Community colleges: most community colleges provide job-finding and resume assistance to anyone who lives in their regional area.

Cover Letters 101

Whether you apply for a job via surface mail or by e-mail, you will need a cover letter to accompany your resume. In a cover letter, a one-page business letter, you will introduce yourself and how your skills are suitable for a job at that company or organization. Cover letters sent via surface mail are more formal than e-mail versions, but in both cases the intent is the same: to get an interview. There are numerous books and Internet resources on writing cover letters. Check the websites listed in the resume section at the beginning of this chapter.

A good cover letter should be succinct, targeted toward the qualifications needed for a particular job, and error free. Do not mass mail generic cover letters—it is generally a complete waste of time. Be sure to focus every cover letter and resume to a job opportunity. Research the company and try to mention something about it in the cover letter. Focus on how your qualifications suit the job opportunity and how you can help the company—not on what they can do for you. You should create one resume and cover letter and tweak it appropriately to each opportunity.

Avoid focusing primarily on your time as a stay-at-home mom in your cover letter, unless the job opportunity is directly relevant to your home-based skills, which may include jobs in the teaching and social services professions. Instead, emphasize how your professional skills, including as a volunteer, qualify you for this job opportunity.

It is important to address the cover letter to the appropriate individual. "To Whom It May Concern" letters (or "Dear Sir or Madam"—*please* avoid this one: this is the twenty-first century!) usually get filed with the hundreds of other resumes and cover letters that a company typically receives.

If the hiring manager is not listed in an advertisement, check out the company's website and then call the company and ask for the name and contact information for the person who is hiring for the job opportunity. If they will not tell you, then you may need to do some sleuthing to find out the manager of a particular department. You can also tap into your networks, including online networks, and see if you can find out who is hiring for the position or at least who is the head of the actual department that is hiring. It's a little extra work, but the results will greatly improve your chance of being considered. If you're not sure if you're sending it to the correct person, send a second copy of the resume and cover letter to the company's personnel office or the general e-mail address listed in the advertisement. In this way, you will cover all your bases.

Resume and Cover Letter Keywords

If you've been out of the workforce for a while, you may be surprised to find that you will need to focus on relevant industry "keywords" in both your resume and your cover letter when applying to jobs at some medium-sized and many larger companies. The "keywords" are words describing functions in a particular job or industry.

Examples of keywords for a Managing Editor might be: editor, management, copyeditor, writer, AP Stylebook, proofreader, HTML, publishing, journalism, budgeting, etc.

If you are responding to an advertisement, include as many keywords as possible, without making the cover letter or resume sound awkward. Why? You need to try to match keywords, because in many cases, especially in large companies, your resume will be downloaded into a central computer. An employee in the company's personnel office will later pull up resumes for candidates to interview on the basis of keyword matches. If your resume does not contain any or enough matching keywords then it may not be retrieved, even if your qualifications are perfect for a job opportunity. Typically, a company will upload only the resumes that best match their keyword search.

While it is impossible to know what the keywords will be for a particular job, your best bet for finding relevant keywords is to study the advertisement and/or look at advertisements for similar opportunities online. Try to identify the skills and experience necessary for a particular job. You can also use a search engine to search "keywords" along with the name of your industry to find relevant keywords. You may want to include different forms of the same word, for example: "editor" and "editing" and both the spelled out and acronyms for a keyword, for example: "Society of Professional Journalists" and "SPJ" or "Associated Press" and "AP." Be sure to use as many keywords as possible that reflect your experience and qualifications.

Online Applications

If you're interested in working at a particular company, go to their website for information on opportunities and how to apply. In many cases, you will be required to fill out their Internet application. You will likely be able to cut-and-paste much of the required information from your resume. Be sure to focus on using industry and job-function keywords, when possible. Address the e-mail cover letter to the hiring official, if at all possible.

After that, don't just sit back and wait for a call. Start networking and try to find someone to put in a good word for you. In order to follow up, you should call the company after seven to ten days to ask about the status of your application. If they say they haven't received your application, ask if you can apply again, and ask for their contact information. Remember this rule for following up:

Be persistent, professional and polite—but do not be a pest!

You may want to follow up by calling back every week to ten days. If you sense that your calls are not welcome, back off and consider sending an occasional e-mail to ask about the status of your application. Follow your intuition. Some hiring managers may be impressed if you're assertive with your job search (but never aggressive or impolite)—while others may be turned off and send you an automatic rejection note. Carefully consider the type of job you are applying for and the reception that you received when you first called to follow up on the job opportunity.

Posting Resumes Online and Privacy

You may want to consider posting your resume online on the "heavy traffic boards" such as CareerBuilder.com, Monster.com, and HotJobs.com, and/or some of the other smaller, niche, and industry boards on the Internet, so that recruiters and hiring managers can find you.

If you post your resume online, be sure to consider the possible privacy ramifications. Always read the "Privacy" section of the website before posting your resume. You may want to consider posting an anonymous resume to hide your identity for the purposes of avoiding identity theft and for overall privacy concerns. You may want to set up a special e-mail address for job-searching purposes only. On some boards, you can post your resume and elect to activate it only when you identify suitable opportunities.

A Few Words about E-mail Netiquette

If you only send e-mails to your spouse and the PTO, you may need to know a few basic rules about e-mail netiquette for job correspondence and for networking purposes. While there is no formal system of e-mail etiquette, no "Emily Post of cyberspace," a few general rules apply that have evolved in the last decade:

1. Always take the time to send a concise, error-free, grammatically correct e-mail.
2. Use correct capitalization.
3. Write clearly. Be sure to get to the point of your e-mail in the first sentence or two.
4. Don't use cutesy acronyms—LOL, BTW, etc.—save it for your teenager.
5. Avoid the smiley faces ☺ and other emoticons—save it for personal correspondence.

6.   Use ordinary fonts like Times Roman and Arial, in black color.
7.   Don't be overly friendly—use Mr. or Mrs., until they reply to you using your first name.
8.   YOU SHOULD NOT SEND E-MAILS IN CAPS, because it is considered impolite, akin to shouting.
9.   Try to reply to e-mails as soon as possible, and not later than twenty-four hours.
10. Use the subject line to clearly identify what the e-mail is about: example: "Applicant: Certified Financial Planner" or "Following Up on Our Meeting Yesterday."
11. Do not mark non-urgent e-mails as urgent—they will typically end up in a spam filter.
12. Do not send attachments, unless requested by or agreed upon by the recipient.

Should You Launch a Website?

Should you launch a website as a job-searching tool? Some job seekers should consider this to showcase professional qualifications, depending on your career objectives. Free and low-cost hosting is available though many Internet service providers. Most of these websites are easy to set up and offer ready made templates for color choices, page layout, etc. Your page will likely become indexed on search engines such as Google, giving you an Internet presence.

While it's desirable for some professionals to set up a website, it would be irrelevant, or even a bit odd, for others to do so. Business owners, consultants, contractual workers, and freelancers may want to set up websites to market their services, and this would not only be appropriate but also expected in these lines of work.

Writers, artists, graphic designers, interior designers, floral arrangers, etc., may also want to set up a website. It can be a virtual "online portfolio" where you showcase your work via photographs and/or links.

Some other professions may be less suitable to setting up a website. If you are looking for a job as an employee at a corporation, for example, then a website may not be your best bet. In your case, consider setting up a page on LinkedIn.com, Spoke.com, Ryze.com, or similar business networking sites.

Blog/Vlog Your Way In

Savvy job seekers may want to consider blogging as a job-search tool. Anyone with good writing skills can set up a blog, which is a personal website with commentary, links to articles, etc., on a particular topic. There are numerous sites for setting up blogs, including Blogger.com and WordPress.com (search "Free Blog sites" on any search engine to find more sites.)

You may want to consider launching a blog as a job-search strategy. For example, if your objective is to re-enter a career in human resources, you might set up a blog in which you track and include news about developments in the industry along with your comments on the topic, also known as "posts." You can include audio "podcasts" on your site, for example, a professional speech you have made that is relevant to your job search. But, unless you are vying for a job as a performer, most career experts advise against creating a video "vlog" or a YouTube video as a job-searching component of your site because it can be seen as both unprofessional and irrelevant to your job search.

Keep in mind that there are a few caveats to consider before setting up your own blog. Successful, high-quality professional blogging is a lot of work. You will need to update it with quality posts at regular intervals. You don't want to start a blog and quit after a short period of time. Your work will be out there for all to see and must be meticulously edited. If you are not a good self editor, then you may need to find someone to edit the blog for you.

As a blogger, you will not make any money on it to start, but may be able to pick up some advertising revenue down the line. Your objective, however, is to use blogging as a platform to become known (or re-known) in your industry and get the job that you are seeking. Blogging can be an excellent way to create your bridge toward the workforce.

Getting Updated References

When you start to hear back from employers who want to set up an interview with you, consider how you will get updated references. It's preferable to get references from professionals who know you well and have worked with you recently, perhaps while you have volunteered. If you left your company in, say, 1998, your reference from a former boss will be "old news." The company may want to speak with that person down the line, especially if they're doing a background check—but the hiring manager won't be impressed.

Still, you may want to contact former bosses and colleagues and ask if they are willing to serve as your reference. Try to get a letter of recommendation to include in your portfolio. If you've kept in touch with them over the years and they are willing, see if they will consider posting an online reference on a business networking site such as LinkedIn.com.

But, while you should try to track down former bosses and colleagues, try to find some newer up-to-date references. Focus on identifying references that have supervised you or worked with you while you were volunteering recently, and ask them if they are willing to serve as your reference.

Onward! To Your Interview

As a job searcher, your interviews should start to roll in if you have concentrated on networking and job searching by traditional and online methods. While job searching may be tedious, the Internet and e-mail enables job applicants to find out about relevant jobs, tailor their resume effectively, and get it to hiring managers almost instantaneously. As a stay-at-home career mom, getting your interview will be your first big hurdle—the second will be on projecting confidence and acing that interview. Find out all the factors necessary for an optimal job interview in Chapter Twelve.

12 HOW TO ACE YOUR INTERVIEW

"It's always been my feeling that God lends you your children until they're about eighteen years old. If you haven't made your points with them by then, it's too late."

—BETTY FORD, FORMER FIRST LADY OF
THE UNITED STATES, (BORN IN 1918)

Batter up! You have volunteered, networked, crafted a resume, researched, and applied for jobs, and now, finally—you are getting requests for interviews. You are almost at home plate—getting a job offer. But first, you need to take the right steps to be confident and energized during your interview. Then you can hit a grand slam.

As a stay-at-home career mom, the critical component of success in interviews is to be self-assured and project confidence in your career decision to stay home with your children. How do you project that confidence? The key to successful interviewing is to: *Hold Your Head High and Don't Apologize.*

You will be confident because you have worked hard at balancing your personal and professional priorities as a stay-at-home career mom. You will know in your heart that you made the right decision for your family and have given your children the gift of your time. Never apologize for staying home! Explain with confidence that you stayed home because it was the best decision for you and your family, and that you are now ready to re-enter the professional work force.

Projecting Confidence

For a successful interview, not only will you need to project confidence about your decision to stay home, but also in your professional qualifications and ability to do the job. You will need to be up-to-date in both technology skills and industry information. You don't want to re-enter the job market like a Rip Van Winkle, wondering why everything has changed. As discussed in previous chapters, you can get current industry information by conducting online and offline research, net-working, and taking classes.

By preparing yourself to re-enter the workforce, you will avoid the situations like that of one woman who went back to work after twelve years and telephoned her husband during her lunch break and said, "Why didn't you tell me there aren't any secretaries anymore?" She was shocked that she had to type her own business correspondence. The first day another mom went back to work, her boss told her to save a document on a Flash Drive—a device that she had never even heard of.

Other moms are surprised by fashion changes ("business casual"), office culture (e-mailing the person in the next cubicle, instead of getting up and walking ten feet to talk to them), and general jargon ("teaming" instead of "team building," in some industries, for example).

Here again is another way that volunteering will pay off. It will give you the opportunity to see changes in the workforce— before you make the transition. It will be less difficult to get hired and an easier transition when you get there. Be sure to also "lurk" (parlance for reading, but not posting) on online industry boards to find out about changes in corporate culture. Networking again is key here. You might consider taking a few friends or former colleagues out to lunch and asking them directly: "What's new in our industry?" and "What do you think I need to know?"

You will also develop confidence by researching a prospective company, which in turn will enable you to express industry and company knowledge during an interview. By learning about the company, you'll be able to ask appropriate questions. It's always a bad move to go into an interview blindly and ask them to tell you about their company. Instead, ask them a question that shows you have done your research; for example, ask them how their business operations have been affected since they expanded their markets into Asia last year, or, how their new product launch is performing so far.

To start, read the company's website and then check Google.com/News for articles that have appeared in the press. While you are on Google.com, use the regular search to search the name of the company and see what hits come up. You can search a metasearch site, such as DogPile.com, to find more search results from a number of search engines.

You should also search the name(s) of the hiring managers you are interviewing to get an idea of their professional background. You can find this information via a search engine and/ or business networking sites such as LinkedIn.com. Use care with how you express this information in your interview. It's appropriate to mention how you read their recent article in an industry publication, but it's not advisable to mention any personal information you inadvertently uncover.

Other information that you will want to research includes annual and financial reports, press releases, etc. You can also check any company you are researching with the Better Business Bureau: BBB.org.

Here are a few links to web pages that focus on how to research companies:

• Learn Web Skills, "Researching Companies Online": LearnWebSkills.com/company/index.html

- New York Public Library, "Searching for Company Information": NYPL.org/research/sibl/company/c2index.htm
- Vault.com

A Typical Interview

In a typical interview, the interviewer will take the time to provide an overview of the company or organization, describe the job that you are interviewing for, and then ask if you have any questions. During this time, you will need to listen attentively and project confidence and professionalism. It's important to maintain eye contact, but not "stare them down." Be careful never to appear bored. Try to appear enthusiastic about the job opportunity.

Watch your body language—your nonverbal gestures during an interview—because you can flub your interview by using inappropriate body language.

There are many facets of projecting a positive body language; here are a few examples:

- Turn off your cell phone before you arrive at your interview.
- Use a firm and confident handshake (not limp, but not aggressive).
- Do not sit before the interviewer sits down.
- Do not slouch in your chair.
- Do not put your hands in your pockets or fold your arms in front of you.
- Do not look at the clock, your watch, or cell phone.
- Lean slightly forward to look interested in the conversation.
- Speak clearly and confidently.

Dress Up for Your Job Interview

It's important to dress professionally for your interview. Unfortunately, that does not mean taking out your business suits that you carefully kept in plastic sleeves for the past decade. Fashions change. Your first step is to try to find out what type of clothing people wear in the organization in which you are interviewing, and then try to dress accordingly. Remember, there are divergent norms for dressing in different types of industries, for example, if you're applying for a banking job then you will need to dress more conservatively than if you are interviewing for a job in advertising.

That said, if you find that the company you are interviewing with has an overall casual dress policy and culture, you will still want to project your respect for the organization by taking the time to "dress up" in professional attire for the interview.

It's advisable to take a look at some business fashion magazines or go to your favorite upscale store to find out what's appropriate. Ask a salesperson to help you during a time when a store is not busy. Some stores may employ personal shoppers, but keep in mind that these services can be expensive. Peruse some business fashion websites. You can also ask your working friends and neighbors for their advice.

This does not necessarily mean that you need to throw out all of your dated business wear, but you may need to do some alterations (think: no more huge shoulder pads) and/or donate some of the items that may now look hopelessly out of style.

Be sure to wear good quality shoes with reasonable heels. You don't want your stilettos stuck in the grates over the street. When dressing, you can express your individuality with an accessory, for example, a colorful silk scarf. Don't go overboard on jewelry—wear one or two nice pieces. Don't wear perfume.

Carefully scrutinize your hair style. If you have not updated your look since high school, take the time to get a new flattering hair cut that will make you feel confident and professional. Get a manicure, but steer clear of bright red polish and flashy types of nails. It's preferable to sport short nails with light pink or clear polish in your interview.

Speaking Confidently

At your interview, be sure to project your confidence, but not arrogance, by speaking clearly. Try not to mumble. For some people, this can be very difficult, because you may feel very nervous. The key to alleviating this nervousness is practice. For most people, interviewing is a learned skill and does not come naturally. Just as you may encourage your children to practice piano, for example, you should practice interviewing.

You can practice interviewing in front of the mirror or by using a tape recorder or video recorder. Or, you may ask your spouse or a friend to role play your interview. It's important to practice many times so that the interview will seem natural to you.

Question Time

One of the key components to practicing how to interview effectively is to learn to anticipate and answer questions and also ask appropriate questions. Generally speaking, many interviewers ask many of the same questions, so you may be able to anticipate these and practice your responses. Be careful not to sound canned when you reply, though. There are many books and websites that contain lists of typical questions. Here are a few examples of general questions and the types of responses that many interviewers are looking for:

1. *Tell me about yourself.*

When you answer this question (or a close variation of it), explain how your education, skills, and qualifications relate to the job. Remember, this is a job interview, not a personal interview, so you should not volunteer any personal information.

2. *Why should I hire you for this job?* Again, state how your education, skills, and qualifications are a perfect fit for the job. Don't mention how the employer can help you, but how you would be an asset to their organization.

3. *What is your biggest accomplishment?* Here you should state something like, "I have had several big accomplishments, but in terms of my professional accomplishments . . ." and describe a professional accomplishment.

4. *What are your short-term career objectives?* By this question, the questioner wants to find out how this job fits in with your

career objectives. They want to ensure that you are not just interviewing for the job because it happened to be advertised.

5. *What are your long-term career objectives?* The reasoning behind this question is the same as #4, but here you will discuss your long-term career goals.

6. *What is your greatest weakness?* Don't answer: "Vanilla Lattes!" (even if it's true.) Here you need to put a positive spin on a the question, for example: "Sometimes I put too much pressure on myself and work too hard," Or, "I am a perfectionist, so I sometimes expect too much from myself and my subordinates." Keep in mind that they may well reply with: "But that sounds like a strength to me," and then ask the same question again. If this happens, be honest, but remember that this answer may cause you to lose the job. A good strategy is to mention something that is not directly relevant to the job opportunity, while at the same time telling the interviewer that you are working to improve on that skill. For example, an applicant for a research job might say that they previously did not feel confident as a public speaker, but have recently joined a public speaking club in the community to try to improve their public speaking skills.

7. *Do you work well under pressure?* Say, "Yes!" (if it's true) and give one or two examples.

8. *What interests you about this company?* Here you will detail what you have learned about the company from your research and explain how you can help the company achieve its goals.

9. *How are you at delegating?* Emphasize that you are a team player and are good at delegating. Provide one or two anecdotes from your past work life or when you were volunteering.

10. *Can you work well in a team?* Again, emphasize that you are a team player. Give one or two anecdotes from your past work life or when you were volunteering.

As a mom re-entering the workforce, you may be asked other questions directly related to your re-entering status, for example:

1. How have you kept your skills up-to-date? This is your key question that may get you the job. Be ready to explain everything you have done to keep up-to-date with your skills.

2. Do you feel comfortable working with a supervisor who may be younger than you? Say: "I'm comfortable working with people of all ages and have been working with people of all ages as a volunteer. My supervisor's age is not relevant to me."

3. How will you handle working while raising children? This question is in the gray area between allowable and illegal questions, depending upon how it's phrased. But, since you will have identified yourself as a transitioning "stay-at-home mom," explain how you have reliable childcare in place and have worked hard at being not only a "stay-at-home mom" but a "stay-at-home *career* mom" by working part-time, consulting, volunteering, owning a home business, or whatever you did. Explain how you don't expect the transition to working full time to be difficult because you have been revving up toward it for some time and are ready to get back into the full-time professional workforce. Re-emphasize how you have maintained and improved your skills and then try to bring the conversation back to how a company will benefit from hiring you because of your specific skill set.

4. Can you travel? You will need to be honest. If you aren't willing to travel, don't apply for positions that state that travel may be required. If you're willing to travel on a limited basis, or with advance notice so you can coordinate your travel plans with your spouse, explain those factors during the interview.

5. Can you work overtime? Here is where your research of family-friendly companies can come into focus. If you already know their policies, then you may be able to answer this question most effectively. If you know that you can't work overtime, or can only work an extra hour because of the hours of your daycare provider, you will need to let them know. If you can coordinate working overtime with your spouse, then explain that in your interview. If you can't stay late, but can work overtime from home on a telecommuting basis, try to focus on that option. Remember that your answer to this question could take you out of the running for the job, but you also may not want to work for such an inflexible employer since your children are your priority.

6. *Do you have childcare arrangements in place?* Interviewers are not supposed to ask this question. For your own sake, however, be sure to make your arrangements or have done all of the research in order to make your childcare decisions before you start interviewing.

7. *What will you do if your child is ill or you need to leave your job?* Again, this is where your research of the family-friendly policies of the company comes into place. You are not advised to work for an employer who would be inflexible in this type of situation. Ideally, they will not ask you this question, but instead explain their flex and family-friendly policies to you in the interview.

8. *How old are your children? Or—how many children do you have?* Employers are not supposed to ask this question. You can just answer the question honestly—or say: "I have several children and already have their childcare arrangements in place." The employer may not know that it's an illegal question. Remember that if you react defensively, then you may not get the job. Your focus should be on how you can do the job and how the number and ages of your children are not relevant to your job performance.

9. *When did you graduate from college?* The employer should not ask you this because asking about your college graduation date may be a way to try to find out your age. You should choose whether to answer the question, but your focus should be on how your age is irrelevant to your job performance, how you have kept up-to-date with technology and your career field, and how you work well with people of all ages.

10. *Are you a single parent?* Employers are not supposed to ask this question. Your employer may be nervous about your childcare arrangements. Answer the question by stating that you are a parent and have reliable childcare and backup childcare arrangements in place. Try to shift the conversation by asking a question about the company.

11. *Why did you leave the workforce?* Say something to the effect: "I felt and still feel that my decision was the best for my family at that time. During my time at home, I maintained my skills and professional qualifications by X, Y, and Z. I am very happy that I had the opportunity to stay home and frankly being a stay-at-home mom enabled me to use important job skills, including management, budgeting, and planning. Multitasking is key to successful stay-at-home parenting (they will probably smile and nod in agreement). But that all said, I am eager to get back to work and am very interested in the possibility of working for your company because I think my skills and background are a perfect fit for this opportunity, because . . ."

12. *Do you think you can leave the workforce for X years without falling behind? What about the parents who stayed at work?* Here you should stress how you kept your skills and qualifications up-to-date. Explain that as a stay-at-home career mom, you did not really leave the workforce entirely, but continued to work, whether as a volunteer, part-timer, business owner, consultant, etc. Emphasize that you have not fallen behind because you have used your own initiative to balance your family and work priorities.

Illegal Questions

Interviewers are not supposed to ask questions or discriminate on the basis of age, birthplace, color, disability, marital status, national origin, pregnancy, race, religion, or sex. Sometimes interviewers ask these questions out of ignorance of the law or out of curiosity or "general friendliness." You can choose to decline to answer the question, or answer it directly or indirectly. In many cases, you may want to try to discern their intent, or what they are really asking, for example, if they ask you about your marital status, are they concerned about backup childcare?

Keep in mind that employers are prohibited by Federal law to ask about childcare arrangements at the pre-employment stage. It is also unlawful to ask if you are pregnant or plan to have more children.

If you feel you have been discriminated against or to find out more about discrimination laws, contact the EEOC at EEOC.gov.

Behavioral Interviewing

Some employers prefer to conduct *behavioral interviews*, where they ask questions to try to find out how you would behave, or react, in certain professional circumstances. Or the interviewer will ask questions to determine how you handled specific situations, with the expectation that past performance predicts future success.

Typical questions relate to an applicant's problem-solving abilities, conflict-resolution techniques, etc. You will need to reply to the questions with detailed examples of how you solved certain problems in the past, whether in the workplace or as a volunteer.

Should you provide examples from your job as a stay-at-home mom? Here you will need to make your own judgment call. For some questions, you may be able to draw on those skills; for example, most moms will have a repertoire of examples of how they solved problems related to multitasking, crisis management, and interpersonal communications.

Again, your best way to have a successful behavioral interview is to prepare beforehand. You should check out websites focused on behavioral interviewing, do comprehensive background research on the company, and try to anticipate and practice your answers before your interview day.

Asking Your Interviewer the Best Questions

At some point in the interview, the interviewer will ask: "Do you have any questions for me?" Your worst responses would be: "No, I think you've covered everything"; any irrelevant or obvious question; or a question that makes it apparent that you have not done your homework about the company. So, while you are doing your research, be sure to make a list of possible questions and tweak them as you find out more about the company. Your best questions will show that you have done your research and have a sincere interest in that company and its operations. Again, the best route to asking questions is to practice. Write down possible questions and practice asking them to your mirror, spouse, or friend. It's likely that you will not be able to ask all of your questions, depending on the flow of conversation in the interview, but you will be adequately prepared to ask the right questions at the right moment.

There are a number of books and Internet resources focus-ing on good interview questions. When accessing these questions, be sure to avoid questions that are too general or sound like they came from a list. Try to personalize your questions to the job opportunity. But, that said, there are several "one-size fits all questions" that you may want to include in your question repertoire:

- Can you describe your ideal candidate for this job?
- Why did the present or last person leave this job?
- Please describe the organizational structure of this department.
- How autonomous is this job? How much interaction will I have with my supervisor(s)?
- What is the greatest challenge of this job?
- How would you expect me to accomplish this goal?
- What are the traits of employees who are most successful in this organization?
- Please describe a typical career path of a professional in this organization.
- What is your management style?
- When should I expect to hear back from you about my candidacy for this position?

Key Tip: Making Sure the Job Is Right for You

Remember in your interview that not only are you being interviewed, but you are also there to find out if this job is right for you. So, when asking questions, be sure to focus on finding out all that you can about the position and company.

Thank You Notes

When you leave your interview, be sure to get the business cards or write down contact information for your interviewer(s). Within twenty-four hours, send a thank you note to them. Use this opportunity to again state how your particular skills and qualifications are a perfect fit for the job. You may want to send both an e-mail thank you note and also a handwritten or typed note by surface mail. In your e-mail message, mention that you have also sent a thank you note by surface mail or dropped it off at their front desk.

If you do choose to hand deliver the thank you note to the front desk of the company, be sure to dress professionally in case you happen to meet up with the interviewer. Your objective is not to run into the interviewer, however, but to get the note to them expediently. Whether you choose to handwrite or type the note is your call. If you have poor handwriting, go for the typed version. And use your intuition, if you are applying for a job in an industry where you think this may be viewed as "old fashioned," type it up and print it out. On the other hand, many people welcome the common courtesy that handwritten thank you notes denote.

If you don't want to further pursue the job opportunity, send an e-mail and politely thank them for their time. Tactfully explain how you don't think your skills are a good fit for this particular job but that you would appreciate it if they would keep you in mind for future opportunities. Why? Because, you never know, a perfect job opportunity may open up for you later, or your interviewer may like and remember you and refer you to a suitable opportunity that they happen to hear about at another company.

Negotiating Work-Life Balance

As a stay-at-home career mom, your priority is always work-life balance. Hopefully, you will have targeted and/or discovered opportunities in companies that share your values. You may be interviewing with companies that enable employees to telecommute, work reduced hours, job share, work on a full-time flexible schedule, etc.

As a job applicant, your best course of action is to first convince your employer that your skills and qualifications are an ideal fit for the job opportunity. Do not mention work-life issues initially because you first want them to want you as an employee. In your interview, focus on how you can benefit the employer, not the other way around.

It's likely that they will mention work-life balance and flexibility in your first or second job interview. If so, follow their lead and ask appropriate questions. If they don't introduce the subject, and you want the job, wait until your second interview to breech the topic. At this point, you will know that they have a serious interest in your candidacy. If you get a negative response, or they are not willing to offer you the job flexibility that you need, then it's a "deal breaker." If so, be thankful that you learned about their inflexibility now, rather than after you have accepted the job. While it may not seem that way initially, it will be their loss, not yours. As a stay-at-home career mom you have worked hard to keep your skills and professional qualifications up-to-date and are a viable employee for companies that share your family values.

And remember that many companies are becoming increasingly flexible not only for ethical reasons, but economic realities. As the massive seventy-seven million Baby Boomers (those born 1946-64) start to retire, there will be an increasing number of vacancies in nearly every industry. Educated, professional moms who have kept their skills up-to-date can fill these jobs and are and will be a needed commodity.

Some of the questions you may want to ask your prospective employer include:

- What is your company's policy for work-life balance? (if it is not included on their website).
- Is work-life balance a priority for your company?
- What percentage of your employees are working parents?
- What types of amenities do you offer to parents?

- How do I find out more a[ ]
  exists) (see Chapter Sever[ ]
- Do you offer telecommut[ ]
  amenable to telecommu[ ]
  (see Chapter Four)
- Are reduced hours or[ ]
  desired) (see Chapter [ ]
- Please describe flexible schea[ ]
  Seven)
- Are employees allowed to work from home on a [ ]
  affected snow day or on a day when their child is sick?
- May employees work flexible schedules or make up time
  if they want to attend activities at their children's school?

Negotiating Pay

When you're interviewing, it's important not to fall into the
trap of accepting any salary just to get a job. If you're in desper-
ate need of a job, you may need to accept a lower salary than
you deserve, but if this is the case, at least try to negotiate,
to the extent possible. In some cases, you may want to take a
job with a lower-than-expected salary as a stepping stone to a
better job. If this is the case, be sure to ask appropriate questions
in your interview about promotion possibilities and typical
career paths.

If you're asked about your expected salary in your interview, try to deflect the question initially with a response such
as: "I don't have a salary in mind yet; I'm first interested in
finding out more about this position." Another good response
might be: "I'm not sure, what is the overall salary range for this
position?" Your goal is to try to avoid answering the question
until you feel you have "sold" yourself to the company and that
they want to hire you. You are then potentially in the "driver's
seat" and may get a higher salary offer than you would have at
the initial stages of your interviewing process.

Be aware that interviewers should not ask you: "What is
the lowest salary that you would accept?" They should not ask
you this question because it could cause some women to accept

han they deserve, particularly vis-à-vis a man
same or comparable job. According to the 2006
, women are paid just 77.3 cents to every $1 paid
for the same or a comparable job. But compensation
nation is unlawful when an employee is paid less
se of her sex—or age, race, color, religon, national origin,
sability. For more information, go to EEOC.gov.

If the interviewer insists that you respond to their request
for your expected salary, make sure you have already done your
research and know the general salary range for the position for
which you are interviewing. Check out sites such as Salary.com,
PayScale.com, GlassDoor.com, SalaryExpert.com, or Vault.
com to get started on your research. Respond with something
similar to: "From my research, I have found that professionals
in this industry earn $60,000 to $67,000. My salary requirements
are negotiable." Then, ask a question and try to direct the conversation back to the job opportunity.

If your interviewer offers you a job at a certain salary,
try to negotiate to the extent possible. According to numerous
studies, women lag far behind men in terms of using their skills
to successfully negotiate salary. Even if you're uncomfortable
negotiating for a better starting salary, negotiating is an
important skill to get what you deserve. It might help to think of
negotiating as finding a better economic deal for your family.

Check out some books and websites on negotiating salary
and practice your techniques before going to the interview. To
start, check out some of the links on this webpage for the University of Wisconsin/Milwaukee's Career Development Center:
UWM.edu/Dept/CDC/jobsearch_preparation_salary.html.

Here are a few tips to get you started:

- If the employer offers you the job at a specific salary, reply:
  "I need to think it over." They may increase their salary
  offer.
- While you are negotiating, follow this rule borrowed from
  the sales arena: "The one who speaks first loses." If they
  offer a certain salary, say, "I see," and then just sit and look

at them. Typically, the interviewer may break the silence and up the salary offer. On the other hand, almost everyone knows this negotiating rule—including your interviewer.

- If you decline the job at a certain salary, then they may up the offer. This is a dangerous game, however, if you want the job, because they may not comply.

Some companies will not have any "wiggle room" and cannot offer you a higher salary. In this case, you may (or may not) be able to negotiate additional benefits. But, if this is your "dream job," carefully consider if you should take it to get your foot in the door. That said, be sure to do your research and be sure that the salary offer is in line with similar jobs in your industry.

As a stay-at-home career mom, avoid sharing your "ancient" salary history. If you have been out of the workforce for a decade, for example, then that number is irrelevant in terms of the current workforce economy. This may play for—or against you—in terms of numbers, so you will need to do your research to find out what salary you should expect.

Remember that you will want to avoid the trap of accepting a low salary because you have been out of the workforce. In some cases, however, this is unavoidable, for example, a teaching position may be compensated solely on the basis of years that you have worked as a teacher.

However, in most cases, focus on what you can do for the company or organization and how your unique and up-to-date professional skills will benefit them to the same extent as another employee who has not left the workforce. As a stay-at-home career mom you will have worked hard to keep yourself in the game. Don't sell yourself short by accepting an entry-level salary, or some sort of "discount" for your time at home.

Taking the First Steps—It's Not a Life Sentence

When you receive a job offer, you will need to carefully evaluate if this is the right opportunity for you in terms of your short-term and long-range career goals. As a mom, you will need to ensure that your needs for work-life balance are satisfied. Think hard about your work-life priorities and actively seek jobs that meet your needs.

It's important to remember that accepting any job is not a life sentence. Most moms will change jobs and perhaps even careers several more times in their lifetime. If you choose to accept this job, and it's not ideal for you, or turns out to be less than you desired, you will be able to take steps to change to another job or career. You may be in a position where you need to take a certain job just to pay the bills. If this is the case, be sure to look for opportunities to use skills that will ultimately transfer to a more ideal job for you in the future.

As stressed throughout this book, your key for success will be building and maintaining your network. Be sure that you don't stop networking once you have a job. Even if you love your job, remember to continue to network actively. Not only will you expand your network of professional contacts, but you will also increase your expertise while becoming known in your industry. By networking, you will always have a team of professional contacts in place if you decide to move to another job or start a business. Networking will enable you to have the contacts necessary to carve out the type of life that you desire— both a career and plenty of time to raise your children.

Finding Work-Life Balance Support

Don't be discouraged if you find it harder than you imagined to transition to the workforce. You may have an ideal job in terms of work-life balance, an understanding boss, a spouse who shares childcare and household responsibilities on an equal basis, excellent childcare and backup care, and a good degree of overall optimism and energy. Or, one or many of these factors may be less than ideal.

You may, for example, find a part-time/reduced-hours job where your boss expects you to work overtime constantly without additional pay, and you find that you are really working full time. Or, you may find telecommuting overwhelming and find it difficult to transition to ordinary home life. Or, your

boss may be using your BlackBerry to
giving you little relaxation at home. C
provider may suddenly move to anot'
number of potential landmines.

238

pro
st

5.

Finding work-life balance supp...
that you can be successful in the workforce and as ..
now full-time working mom, consider joining a working mom...
group in your community where you can commiserate and find
solutions to work-life problems. Some larger companies have
support groups for working parents. You can also contribute
to relevant Internet discussion boards and websites focused on
work-life issues. Many national organizations focus on work-
life balance. Here are just a few examples:

- Alliance for Work-Life Progress: AWLP.org
- Families and Work Institute: FamiliesAndWork.org
- Work and Family Connection: WorkFamily.com
- World at Work: WorldAtWork.org

Get a Life! Ten Tips for an Ideal Work-Life Balance

Life may be a lot more frazzled when you start back to work. After
a transition period, you should be able to set up a routine that
will enable you to have an ideal work-life balance. One teacher
who went back to work after many years at home said the first
year was "extremely difficult and stressful." But, after that, she
said balancing parenting and working was "smooth sailing."
Here are a few tips to get your work-life balance priorities on
course and maintain them throughout your career.

1. Try to be 100 percent at work emotionally when you are at
   work, and 100 percent at home when you are home. Work/
   home lines can be blurry. Try to make the distinction.
2. Work as a team with your spouse. Divide all childcare,
   cleaning, chores, errands, etc., equitably.
3. Streamline chores and family responsibilities, for example:
   take one run rather than several trips to several stores.
4. Set up backup childcare plans in advance. If your childcare

ider calls in sick, have a plan in place for who will
ay with your children.

Focus on your health: Make sleep a priority. You cannot
have a positive work-life balance if you are exhausted.
Focus on nutrition and getting regular exercise.

6.   Set up a schedule. Easygoing moms may have been flexible
on bedtimes, meal times, etc. Now you will need to set up
a regular household schedule.

7.   Drop unnecessary activities. Your children do not need
to be in multiple activities. You and your children will be
exhausted if you sign up for too many activities. Some
families allow their children to take one sport per season.
Others have different rules. Sit down with your children
and come up with a workable activities schedule.

8.   Go on a regular date night with your spouse, perhaps
twice a month.

9.   Take a family vacation yearly, if possible. Relax and turn
off your cell phone. You will have earned it.

10.   Drop the guilt. There is no perfect work-life balance set
up and everyone's needs are different. As a stay-at-home
career mom, you are trying your best to "have it all."
Make it a priority for you or your spouse to attend all
of your children's activities and school functions, but if it
is sometimes impossible, remember that you have tried
your best.

Good Parenting Lasts Forever

Professional career success is important for many people,
including many stay-at-home moms. We also need to have
an income. Parenting, however, lasts forever. Your good
parenting decisions will pass on to your children and your
children's children. Whether you choose to be a stay-at-home
mom exclusively, work full-time, volunteer, work part-time,
telecommute, run a business, or work as a consultant or
freelancer, is a decision that only you can make.

The purpose of this book is to let you know that you have
options and point you in the direction of how to find out more

about those types of opportunities. For most of us, gone are both the stereotypical 1950s' days (dad at work, mom at home baking cookies) and the 1980s' days (mom and dad at work fifty hours a week, children in daycare full time).

Today, working parents have additional options. The Internet has opened a whole new world for job flexibility. All moms work, but it is your own choice on if, how, and when you want to work. In the words of Grandma Moses, the American folk artist: "Life is what we make it, always has been, always will be."

AFTERWORD: A FEW
ADDITIONAL COMMENTS

"I looked on childrearing not only as a work of love and
duty but as a profession that was fully interesting and
challenging as any honorable profession in the world and
one that demanded the best that I could bring to it."
—Rose Kennedy (1890–1995), mother of former
U.S. president John F. Kennedy

Your career path does not have to go in a straight line.
Sometimes you will purposefully veer off the traditional
route of working full time and forge a new career direction.
Later you may elect to return to working full time. As a stay-
at-home career mom, your future may include staying home
exclusively, working full time, volunteering, working part-
time, telecommuting, owning a business, consulting, and
freelancing.

Flexibility is the key to short-term and long-range career
success. Both employees and their employers need to embrace
flexibility as a priority. Work-life balance is important to all
employees, women and men, parents and nonparents. With the
advent of Internet technology, many employees no longer need

to be chained to their desk. Not only can many employees work from home on a telecommuting basis, but also work in general can get done much faster and more efficiently by means of the Internet and computer technology.

In today's society, it seems ridiculous to log seventy to eighty hour workweeks. Proving your professional worth by working twelve-hour days is a relic of the 1980s—and should be quickly tossed into the "Do you remember when . . . ?" category of conversation. An efficient full-time employee should be able to get their work done within the confines of a regular forty-hour timeframe, barring exceptional circumstances, and in certain (but very few) professions. Some employees may want to work overtime, for example, commissioned salespersons; but then it should be an option, not a requirement, for that employee.

Working parents should be able to leave at the hour designated by their work schedule, perhaps 5 p.m., without working overtime, except in occasional, extraordinary, and/ or non-expected cases—and still be viewed as a dedicated employee who is as equally on track for promotions as their colleagues. We have all seen slacker employees who work overtime by just sitting at their desk, looking busy while doing nothing, so they can be seen as a motivated employee by their boss and colleagues. Other employees do not get their work done on time because they are disorganized, off task, or spend too much time at the water cooler.

A societal workplace paradigm shift is needed. Employers should evaluate employees solely on the basis of performance, not hours clocked on the job. If the work cannot get done by a dedicated and diligent employee, then perhaps the employer is expecting the employee to do the work of two professionals and should hire an additional employee.

Professional Moms Are in the Driver's Seat

As a stay-at-home career mom, you are in the "driver's seat." Employers need you. As the seventy-seven million Baby Boomers start to retire, their jobs will need to be filled. Some employers are now trying to woo stay-at-home moms back into the workforce, and more employers will likely follow their lead. There is a wealth of educated women who choose to stay home, and they should have many opportunities if they want to re-enter the workforce.

A Simple Solution

Working moms should continue to demand more flexibility in the workplace. Companies should be encouraged to consider "nontraditional" scheduling for filling the mass of projected vacancies. When possible, working moms should be allowed to work flexible schedules that start early in the day, generally at some time between 6:00-8:00 a.m.

A simple solution to lure professional moms back into the workplace—and keep them there—is to establish workplace setups in which some working moms could be hired to work full time from September-June, on the same "permanent hire" basis as a regular full-time year-around employee, much like educators, but have the summer off and/or telecommute from home from June-August. As a permanent hire for the company, these employees would be contractually obligated to return to working full time in September.

But is this just Utopia for working moms? In many cases, it does not have to be. Depending upon the job and responsi-bilities, companies could purposefully design some positions that have a downtime during the summer months. "Summers off" jobs would work best with jobs that are relatively inde-pendent in scope. Of course the world cannot just shut down in the summer—and this job setup would not work in customer-oriented jobs or many medical jobs, for example. And companies could not allow all of its employees to take the summer off, but would need to decide on a case-by-case basis.

But, it might work well; for example, an employee might have a computer-based design project that is scheduled for completion in June. The next project could start up again in September. During the summer, they could telecommute from home, perhaps part-time, to organize the specifics for setting up the next project. Other examples might include:

an environmental scientist who does a research study that is purposefully scheduled from September-June; a lawyer who is assigned cases that are projected to be completed by the end of Spring, and then does research during the summer on a telecommuting basis; or a magazine writer who writes additional monthly articles during the period before the summer break and other articles on a telecommuting basis from home during the summer.

In each of these cases, their pay would need to be reduced proportionally if they reduce their hours or do not work at all during the summer—but for same working moms, it would be worth it. Employees would still be eligible for health and other benefits, and the employee would not be penalized professionally for scheduling their summer downtime. Contractual "summer off" positions would be deemed of equal professional caliber to those held by employees who work on a twelve-month schedule—not so-called "Mommy Track" jobs with lower levels of responsibility.

Employers would benefit from setting up these types of contractual "summer off" professional opportunities too, because they could fill their position with talent that they would not be able to get if they did not offer a flexible schedule. If a company routinely has periods of downtime, then they could schedule those periods accordingly for working moms, and not have to pay an employee for times when there is little or no available work. Companies could reduce their need to obtain employees via outsourcing.

This type of job setup would be similar to working as a professor at a university. During the academic year, professors are required to teach their students and engage in other related academic duties. During the summers, many professors typically aren't required to provide "face time" (unless they are teaching summer classes) but work by conducting research, writing, engaging in professional speaking, etc., and preparing for the next school year. Many other types of jobs can be designed using this professorial model. The employee's main project or duties would be purposefully scheduled to wrap up in June and to start again in September. Planning and preparation for the next work cycle could be done on a telecommuting basis from home during the summer months.

Flexibility needs to be a priority in America's workplace for both women and men. For working parents, flexibility is the critical component of successfully balancing parenting while continuing their professional career. It is also a gift to their children, who will spend more time with their less-frenzied parents, and who will not need to spend entire summers every year in daycare centers. Employers will have more efficient, happier employees—and be able to lure back some of the 5.6 million stay-at-home moms into their workplaces. Everyone wins.

Charting Your Career Course

As you chart your career course into the future, remember that you have many choices to consider for work options. You can return to the professional workforce or continue to be a stay-at-home career mom and use your education and experience in creative ways—perhaps by setting up a business or opening a consultancy. Or, you can work part-time or telecommute. All of these options are valuable work experiences and are equal in caliber to the experiences of those moms who choose to work full time. All moms work, but only *you* can decide which way to navigate your road ahead.

ABOUT THE AUTHOR

STATESIDER PHOTOGRAPHY

Sharon Reed Abboud is a writer specializing in career issues. She has written articles about careers and higher education for Quintessential Careers (QuintCareers.com), the *Washington Post Express*, *Succeed Magazine*, Back2 College.com, and others. Her online articles have been linked by many sites of interest to career seekers. Sharon also answers questions as a career-planning expert for AllExperts.com and was an academic advisor and a career specialist at the American University, in Washington, D.C. Born in New York City, Sharon lives in Northern Virginia with her husband and four children. Sharon is a stay-at-home career mother—she balances raising her children with being a full-time writer.